BLOOM

Founded by | arihant

AF673827

Olympiad ACE

A Comprehensive Practice Book

for School Olympiads & Talent Search Exams

SCIENCE

Class 9

by

Anam Arzoo & Suresh Sharma

Olympiad ACE

BLOOM

Bloom Cap Edu Ventures Pvt. Ltd.

卐 **Administrative & Production Office**

'Ramchhaya' 4577/15, Agarwal Road, Darya Ganj, New Delhi -110002
Tele: 011- 47630600, 43518550

卐 **PRICE:** ₹125.00

Published by Arihant Publications (I) Ltd.

For further information about the books log on to
www.bloomcap.org

Follow us on

Preface

"Future belongs to those Who prepares for it today"

School Olympiads are National & International level competitions conducted by different Government, Non-Government & Educational Organisations with the purpose of making the children ready to face competitive exams.

The challenging Questions asked in Olympiads motivate them to learn more & more and bring out the best result with improved academic performance. The Awards & Scholarship offered by Olympiads motivate children to aspire & strive for doing better and emerge out to be the best.

Science Olympiads

Being a Scientist or Engineer or Doctor has always been a dream of each school going child. A good command over Science is a must for any of these. Questions of Science Olympiads are structured to help students to develop scientific temperament & motivate them to understand the concepts of science. They also focuses on improving existing knowledge of a student by adding more information.

'Bloom Science Olympiad Study Book Class 9' is a perfect resource to Study & Practice for Olympiad Exams and other National & State Level Talent Search Exams & Other Competitions.

Some Special Features of Bloom Science Olympiad Study Books are;

- Chapterwise Exercises having different types of Objective Questions; Analytical, Applications, Remembering etc, at par with the Olympiad Level.
- Detailed Explanation for each question.
- Olympiad Pattern Practice Sets at the end.

This book is prepared by Expert Panel with the utmost care, still if you have any suggestions regarding its improvement then feel free to contact us at support@bloomcap.org. We will try to inculcate your suggestions in the further editions.

Contents

01. Matter in Our Surroundings 1-5

02. Is Matter Around Us Pure? 6-9

03. Atoms and Molecules 10-14

04. Structure of the Atom 15-20

05. The Fundamental Unit of Life 21-29

06. Tissues 30-36

07. Motion 37-40

08. Force and Laws of Motion 41-45

09. Gravitation 46-48

10. Work and Energy 49-53

11. Sound 54-57

12. Improvement in Food Resources 58-64

- Practice Set 1 65-72
- Practice Set 2 73-80
- Hints & Solutions 81-108

Chapter 01

Matter in Our Surroundings

1 Mark Questions

1. Consider the following experimental set up.

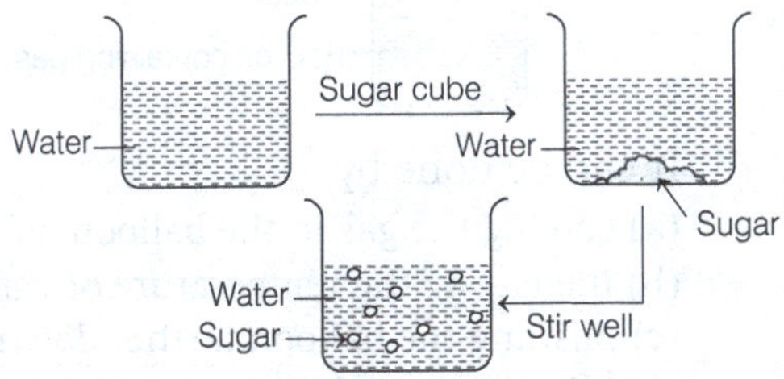

The conclusions obtained from the above experiment are

I. nature of matter is continuous.
II. matter is made up of tiny particles.
III. particles of sugar occupy the spaces present in between the particles of water.

The correct statements are

(a) I and II (b) II and III
(c) III and I (d) All of these

2. Some of the substances are given below.

I. Air II. Water
III. Sand IV. Butter

Arrange these substances in increasing order of kinetic energy of individual molecules.

(a) III < IV < II < I
(b) IV < III < II < I
(c) III < IV < I < II
(d) IV < III < I < II

3. A 50 cm ^{3} sample of alcohol is mixed with 50 cm ^{3} of water.

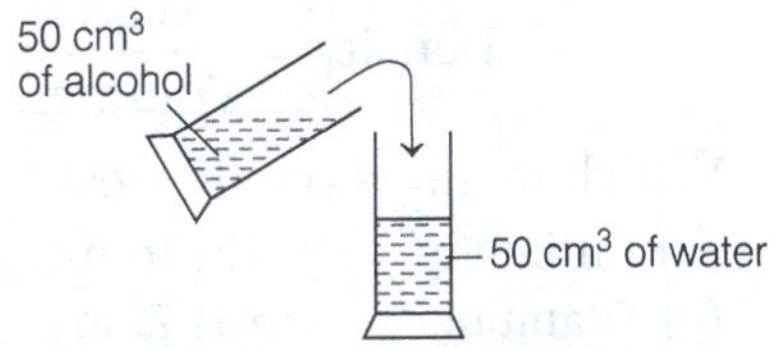

The volume of the mixed alcohol and water is found to be 97 cm ^{3}.
Which of the following is the best explanation?

(a) Alcohol molecules fit into gaps between water molecules
(b) Some alcohol molecules evaporate
(c) Water and alcohol react to form a gas which escapes
(d) Water and alcohol react to produce a salt which then dissolves

4. In which of the following conditions, the distance between the molecules of hydrogen gas increases in container?

I. Increasing the volume of container of hydrogen gas.
II. Increasing the number of molecules of hydrogen gas.

Choose the correct option.

(a) Only I (b) Only II
(c) Both I and II (d) Neither I nor II

5. An equal mass of four different metals was mixed together to form an alloy. The graph shows the proportions by volume of each of these metals.

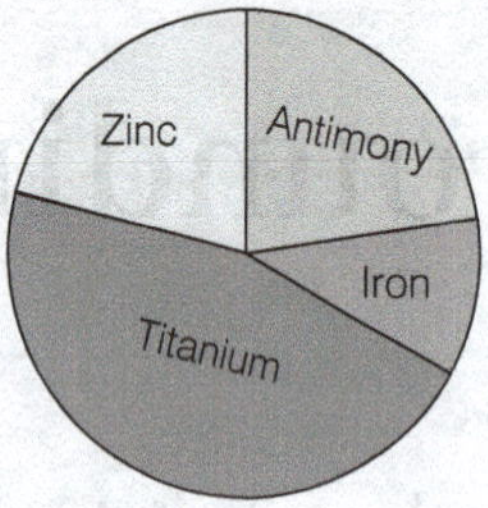

The density of an object is given as

$$\text{Density} = \frac{\text{Mass}}{\text{Volume}}$$

Which metal is the densest?

(a) Antimony (b) Iron
(c) Titanium (d) Zinc

6. A few substances are arranged in the increasing order of 'forces of attraction' between their particles. Which one of the following represents a correct arrangement?

(a) Water, air, wind
(b) Air, sugar, oil
(c) Oxygen, water, sugar
(d) Salt, juice, air

7. The table given below shows the melting and boiling points of four pure substances.
At room temperature, which substance is a liquid and rapidly evaporates, if left exposed to air?

Substance	Melting point/°C	Boiling point/°C
A	−100	−35
B	−7	58
C	−6	225
D	44	280

The correct answer is

(a) *A* (b) *B*
(c) *C* (d) *D*

8. For an ideal gas, number of moles per litre in terms of its pressure p, gas constant R and temperature T is

(a) pT/R (b) pRT
(c) p/RT (d) RT/p

9. We need to increase the volume of the gas in the balloon as shown in the diagram given below.

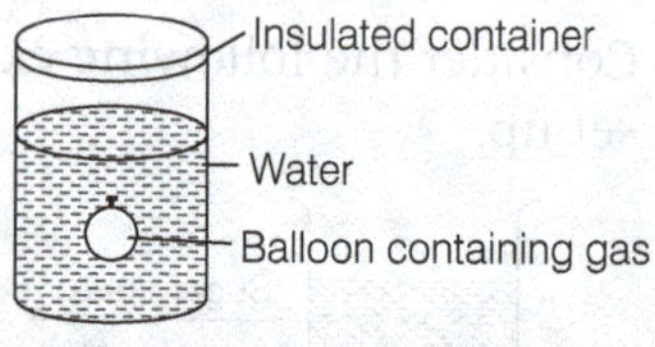

It can be done by

(a) cooling the gas in the balloon only
(b) increasing the temperature of water
(c) pushing the balloon farther down into the water bath
(d) closing the tap of the water bath

10. The given figure shows graph of pressure (p) *versus* density (d) for an ideal gas at two temperatures T_1 and T_2.

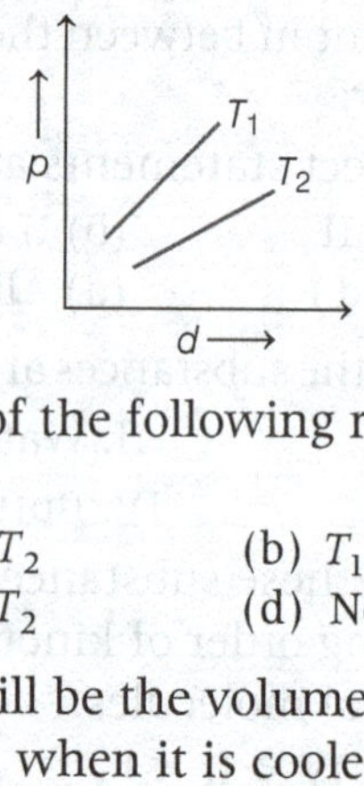

Which of the following relation is true?

(a) $T_1 > T_2$ (b) $T_1 = T_2$
(c) $T_1 < T_2$ (d) None of these

11. What will be the volume of 600 cm^3 of a gas, when it is cooled from 27° C to 7° C?

(a) 380 cm^3 (b) 420 cm^3
(c) 560 cm^3 (d) None of these

12. The cover plate was removed from the gas jars shown in the diagram. After several days, the colour of the gas was same in both jars.

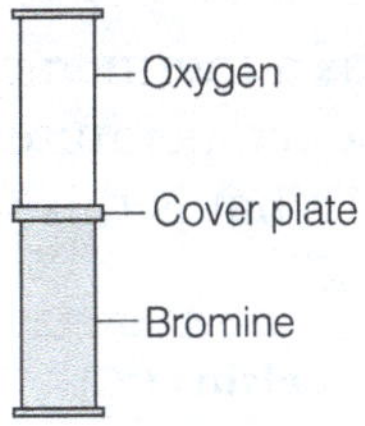

Which one of the following statements explain this change?

(a) Oxygen and bromine gases have equal densities
(b) Oxygen and bromine molecules are in random motion
(c) Oxygen and bromine molecules diffuse at the same rate
(d) Equal volumes of oxygen and bromine contain equal number of molecules

13. Look at the following figures and suggest in which of the vessels *A*, *B*, *C* or *D*, the rate of evaporation will be the highest?

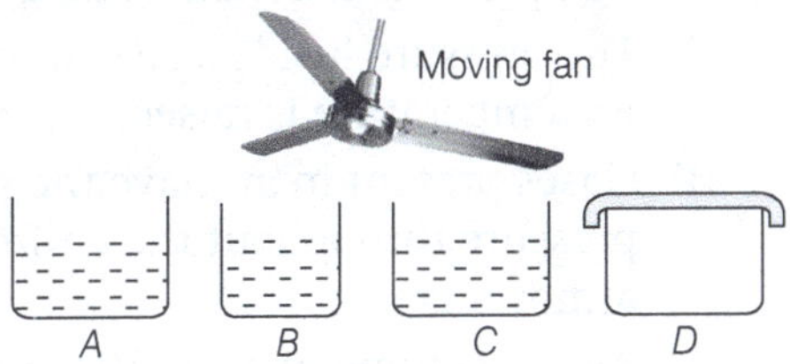

(a) *A* (b) *B*
(c) *C* (d) *D*

14. The diagram shows some of the changes of state.

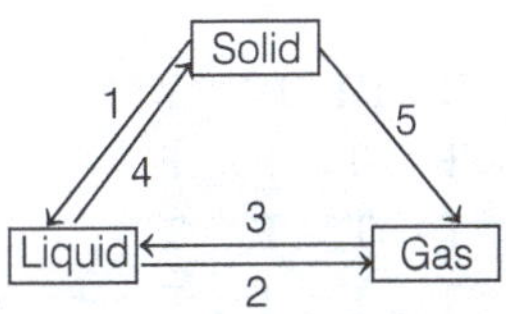

Which statement is correct about the diagram?

(a) Although the change is not shown on the diagram, a gas can change directly to a solid
(b) The changes 1 and 3 involve particles moving close together
(c) The changes 2 and 4 involve particles moving further apart
(d) The changes 3, 4 and 5 all involve the release of energy

15. The conical flask contains compound *X* which is present in solid, liquid and gaseous states.

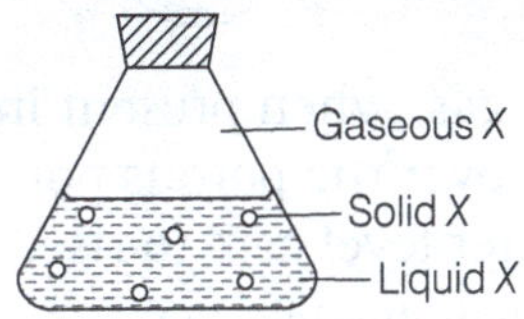

Which of the following statement is correct?

(a) A gaseous *X* molecule has a lower mass than a liquid *X* molecule
(b) Energy is released when *X* changes from liquid to solid
(c) Liquid *X* is at a higher temperature than solid *X*
(d) Liquid *X* molecules vibrate about fixed position

16. A gas present in a sealed cylinder is heated.

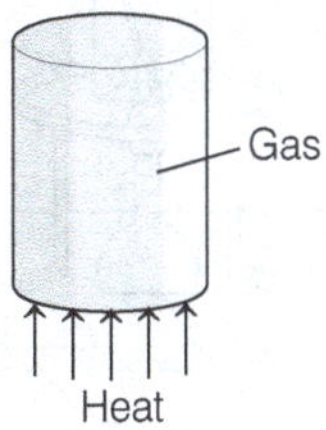

Which of the following does not increase as the gas is heated?

(a) The average number of gas molecules hitting the cylinder walls per second
(b) The average kinetic energy of the gas molecules
(c) The average speed of the gas molecules
(d) The average distance between the gas molecules

2 Marks Questions

17. The diagram shows a diffusion experiment.

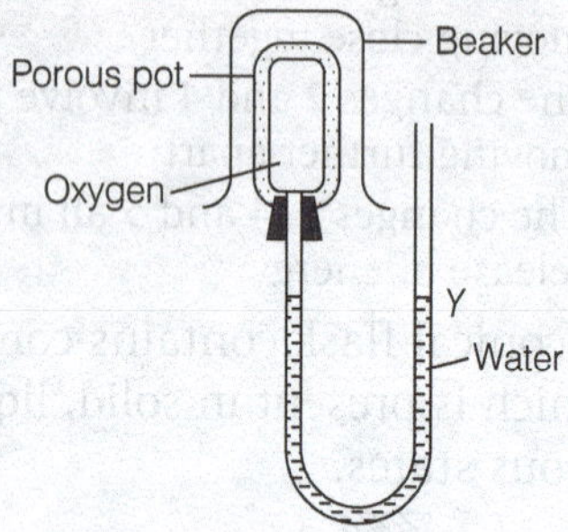

Which gas, when present in the beaker over the porous pot, will cause the water level at *Y* to rise?

(a) Carbon dioxide (CO_2)
(b) Chlorine (Cl_2)
(c) Methane (CH_4)
(d) Nitrogen dioxide (NO_2)

18. Sneha set up the experiment for melting of ice in a beaker and noted down the temperature throughout the process.

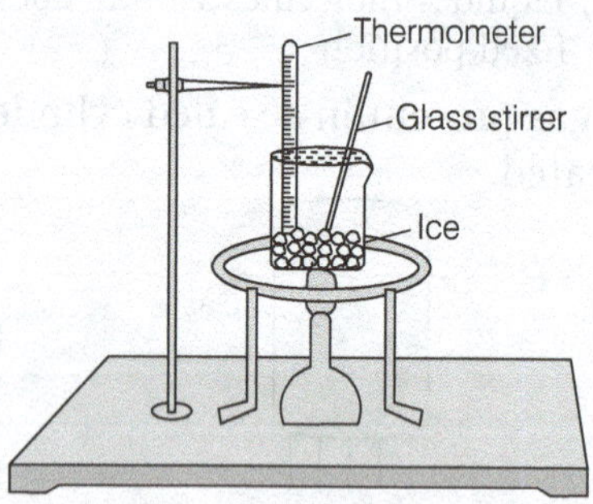

What do you think she observed when the ice was melting?

(a) The temperature in the thermometer kept increasing till the whole ice melted
(b) Once the melting process started, the temperature in thermometer remains constant though the heating was on
(c) There was no change in temperature throughout the experiment
(d) Ice did not melt on heating. It was converted to vapours

19. Jack has a thermometer which shows that the temperature of a substance is 180 °F. What is this temperature in °C and in K?

	Celsius (°C)	**Kelvin** (K)
(a)	82	280
(b)	150	280
(c)	82	355
(d)	150	355

20. If 5.52×10^{-2} moles of a gas occupies 413 mL at 88°C, the pressure (in atm) is

(a) 2 (b) 4
(c) 8 (d) 10

21. State [T] for True and [F] for False.

I. The gas which obeys gas laws under all the conditions of temperature and pressure is called a real gas.
II. The pressure inside a sealed tube, if its temperature is raised, increases.
III. Gases present in air have the same pressure throughout the entire atmosphere.
IV. As the volume of a specific amount of gas, at 27°C, decreases, its pressure decreases.
V. Making of chapati is an application of Charles' law.

Codes

	I	II	III	IV	V
(a)	T	F	T	F	F
(b)	F	T	T	F	T
(c)	F	T	F	F	F
(d)	T	T	T	F	F

22. Match the law given in Column I with the constant condition given in Column II and choose the correct answer using the codes given below the columns.

	Column I		Column II
A.	Boyle's law	1.	Temperature
B.	Charles' law	2.	Pressure
C.	Avogadro's law	3.	Pressure and temperature
D.	Ideal gas equation	4.	Number of moles

Codes

	A	B	C	D		A	B	C	D
(a)	4	3	2	1	(b)	1	2	3	4
(c)	1	3	2	4	(d)	4	3	1	2

23. Which of the following graphs represent(s) Boyle's law correctly?

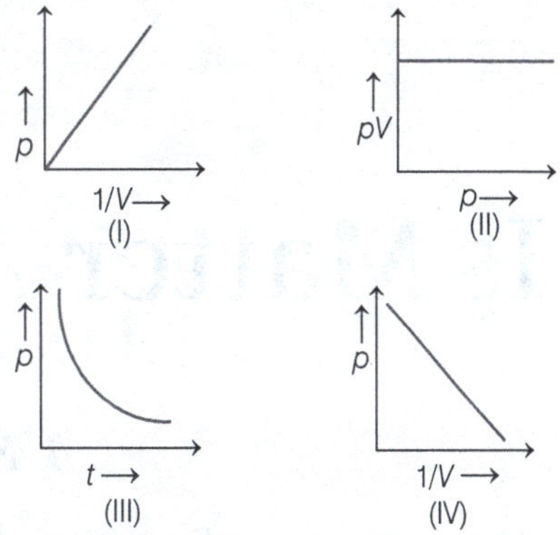

(a) (I), (II) and (III)
(b) (I) and (IV)
(c) (II) and (III)
(d) (I), (II) and (IV)

Chapter 02

Is Matter Around Us Pure?

1 Mark Questions

1. The electronic configuration of an element *M* is 2, 8, 3. On this basis, the nature of oxide of element *M* is

(a) acidic
(b) basic
(c) amphoteric
(d) data insufficient

2. Which list contains three elements that all exist as diatomic molecules at room temperature?

(a) Hydrogen, fluorine, neon
(b) Nitrogen, chlorine, neon
(c) Nitrogen, oxygen, fluorine
(d) Oxygen, chlorine, helium

3. Mayank takes two elements *X* and *Y*. The elements *X* and *Y* combine to give a product *Z*. The correct statement about *Z* is

(a) *Z* has more mass than that of *X*
(b) *Z* has less mass than that of *X*
(c) *Z* has less mass than that of *Y*
(d) *Z* show same properties as that of *X* and *Y*

4. A solution contains 40 g of common salt in 320 g of water. The concentration in terms of mass by mass percentage of solvent is

(a) 11% (b) 89% (c) 10% (d) 99%

5. A solution contains 50 g of common salt in 450 g of water. Calculate the concentration in terms of mass by mass percentage of solution.

(a) 10% (b) 20%
(c) 30% (d) 40%

6. 100 g of water can hold 0.1 kg of a substance *X*. Ravi wants to prepare a saturated solution of substance *X*. For this, he added 90 g of *X* to 0.1 kg of water. What did he get?

(a) A saturated solution
(b) An unsaturated solution
(c) A supersaturated solution
(d) A dilute solution

7. Consider the following statements about Tyndall effect.

I. It is scattering and polarising of light by small suspended particles.
II. It is due to dispersion of light.
III. It is due to refraction of light.
IV. It is the *zig-zag* motion of suspended particles.

The true statement(s) is/are

(a) Only I
(b) II and IV
(c) Only III
(d) Only II

8. Tyndall effect can be observed in a colloidal solution.

Consider light scattering in the following.

I. When sunlight passes through the canopy of a dense forest.
II. When normal light passes through copper sulphate solution.
III. When normal light passes through milk.
IV. When a fine beam of light enters a room through a small hole.

Choose the correct option.

(a) I and IV
(b) I, III and IV
(c) II and III
(d) III and IV

9. The processes which involve physical as well as chemical changes are

I. burning of a candle.
II. rusting of an iron nail.
III. sublimation of ammonium chloride.
IV. dissolving salt in water.
V. crystallisation of copper sulphate.

Codes

(a) I and II
(b) I and III
(c) III and IV
(d) II and V

10.

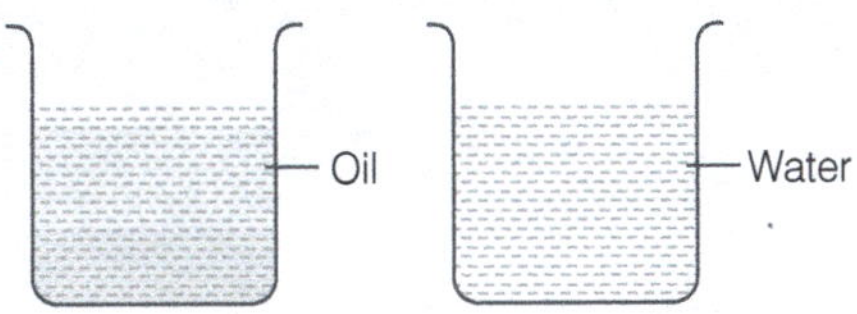

Ravi tested both the above liquids and found that these two differ in their odour as well as in inflammability. The former one is highly inflammable while the other is used to extinguish fire. It is due to the change in their

(a) density
(b) chemical composition
(c) melting point
(d) boiling point

11. State [T] for True and [F] for False.

I. Germanium, arsenic and antimony possess some properties of metals and some properties of non-metals.
II. Hydrogen (H_2), oxygen (O_2) and nitrogen (N_2) are elements.
III. All homogeneous substances are pure.
IV. Mercury and bromine are the only two liquid elements.

Codes

	I	II	III	IV		I	II	III	IV
(a)	T	T	F	T	(b)	F	T	F	F
(c)	T	F	F	T	(d)	F	T	F	T

12. Match the solutions given in Column I with their types given in Column II and choose the correct answer using the codes given below the columns.

Column I	Column II
A. Alcohol + water	1. Gas in liquid
B. Amalgamated zinc	2. Solid in liquid
C. Aqueous solution of sodium chloride	3. Liquid in liquid
D. Aerated water	4. Liquid in solid
	5. Solid in solid

Codes

	A	B	C	D		A	B	C	D
(a)	3	4	2	1	(b)	3	5	2	1
(c)	3	5	1	2	(d)	3	2	4	1

13. **Statement I** A solution having more amount of solute than the saturated concentration is called a supersaturated solution.

Statement II Supersaturated solutions are stable at room temperature.

Which of the following statement(s) is/are true?

(a) Only I (b) Only II
(c) Both I and II (d) Neither I nor II

14. Match the processes given in Column I with the type of change given in Column II and choose the correct answer using the codes given below the columns.

Column I	Column II
A. Rusting of iron	1. Physical as well as chemical
B. Melting of wax	2. Chemical
C. Burning of candle	3. Physical
D. Baking of cake	4. No change

Codes

	A	B	C	D		A	B	C	D
(a)	4	3	1	2	(b)	2	3	1	4
(c)	1	2	3	1	(d)	2	3	1	2

15. Consider the following statements about chemical change.

I. Change in colour only
II. Change in temperature only
III. Evolution of gas only
IV. Evolution of water only

Codes

(a) Only I
(b) Only I and III
(c) I, II and III
(d) Only IV

16. State [T] for True and [F] for False.

I. Making of wine from grapes is a chemical change.
II. A chemical change has no effect on physical properties but changes only the chemical composition.
III. A physical change has no effect on chemical composition but affect only physical properties.
IV. Drying of paint on a door is a physical change.
V. Electrolysis of water by passing electric current through it, is a chemical change.
VI. Evaporation is a chemical change while decantation is a physical process.

Codes

	I	II	III	IV	V	VI
(a)	T	T	T	F	F	F
(b)	F	T	T	T	F	T
(c)	T	F	F	F	T	T
(d)	T	F	T	F	T	F

2 Marks Questions

17. Match the type of colloid given in Column I with their examples given in Column II and choose the correct answer using the codes given below the columns.

Column I	Column II
A. Gel	1. Rubber
B. Foam	2. Face cream
C. Emulsion	3. Coloured gemstone
D. Solid sol	4. Butter
E. Aerosol	5. Cloud

Codes

	A	B	C	D	E
(a)	1	2	4	5	3
(b)	2	1	3	4	5
(c)	4	1	2	3	5
(d)	3	4	5	1	2

18. Two chemical species X and Y combine together to form a product P which contains both X and Y.

$$X + Y \longrightarrow P$$

X and Y cannot be broken down into simpler substances by simple chemical reactions. Which of the following concerning the species X, Y and P are correct?

I. P is a compound.

II. X and Y are compounds.

III. X and Y are elements.

IV. P has a fixed composition.

Codes

(a) I, II and III
(b) I, II and IV
(c) II, III and IV
(d) I, III and IV

19. Match the Column I with Column II and select the correct option below.

Column I	Column II
A. Substance consists of only a single type of constituent particles	1. Heterogeneous mixtures
B. Visible boundaries of separation between its constituents	2. Compound
C. Constituents lose their properties	3. Mixture
D. Chemical reaction does not takes place during its formation.	4. Metal

Codes

	A	B	C	D		A	B	C	D
(a)	1	2	3	4	(b)	4	3	1	2
(c)	4	1	2	3	(d)	2	3	1	4

20. State [T] for True and [F] for False.

I. A homogeneous liquid which on boiling leaves a solid residue is a solution containing solid as solute.

II. All solutions are mixtures but all the mixtures are not solutions.

III. Solution of copper sulphate will exhibit Tyndall effect.

IV. Sugar mixed in water is an example of heterogeneous mixture.

V. Like solids, solubility of gases also increases with increase in temperature.

VI. Mechanical stirring increases the solubility.

Codes

	I	II	III	IV	V	VI
(a)	F	F	T	T	F	F
(b)	T	F	T	F	T	F
(c)	T	T	F	F	F	T
(d)	F	T	T	T	F	F

Chapter 03

Atoms and Molecules

1 Mark Questions

1. The formula of chloride of a metal M is MCl_3, then the formula of the phosphate of metal M will be

(a) MPO_4 (b) M_2PO_4
(c) M_3PO_4 (d) $M_2(PO_4)_3$

2. Nitrogen forms several oxides like NO, N_2O, NO_2, N_2O_4, N_2O_3, N_2O_5. The law of definite proportions is not applicable to the oxides of nitrogen because

(a) atomic weight of nitrogen is not constant
(b) molecular weight of nitrogen is variable
(c) equivalent weight of nitrogen is variable
(d) atomic weight of oxygen is variable

3. Sohan predicted that 0.220 g of a gas when filled in a vessel; occupy 112 mL at a pressure of 1 atm and temperature of 273 K. The gas can be

(a) nitrogen dioxide (b) nitrous oxide
(c) carbon dioxide (d) propene

4. The formula of carbonate of a Metal P is PCO_3, then the formula of the fluoride of Metal P will be

(a) PF_3 (b) PF
(c) PF_2 (d) P_2F_3

5. When carbon and sulphur combine, they form a compound with the formula CS_2. This compound is known by the name carbon disulphide.

In carbon disulphide (CS_2), the mass of sulphur in combination with 3.0 g of carbon is

(a) 4.0 g (b) 6.0 g
(c) 64.0 g (d) 16.0 g

6. Four students A, B, C and D verified the law of conservation of mass by performing chemical reaction between barium chloride and sodium sulphate.

All of them took 107.2 g barium chloride solution and 116.1g of sodium sulphate solution and mixed them in the beaker of mass 150 g. They reported their results as follows

Student	Colour of reaction mixture after mixing	Mass of reaction mixture in the beaker including mass of beaker
A	White ppt.	383.3g
B	Brown ppt.	393.3g
C	White ppt.	373.3g
D	Brown ppt.	363.3g

The correct observation is that of student

(a) *A* (b) *B*
(c) *C* (d) *D*

7. Two gaseous samples were analysed.

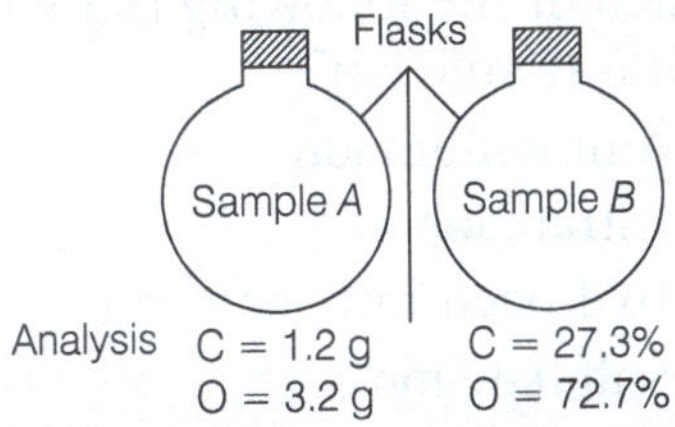

The experimental data are in accordance with which of the following laws of combination?

(a) Law of conservation of mass
(b) Law of definite proportions
(c) Law of reciprocal proportions
(d) Law of multiple proportions

8. If 6.3 g of $NaHCO_3$ is added to 15.0 g of CH_3COOH solution, the residue is found to weigh 18.0 g. What is the mass of CO_2 released in this reaction?

(a) 4.5 g (b) 3.3 g
(c) 2.6 g (d) 2.8 g

9. An organic compound, consisting of carbon, hydrogen, nitrogen and oxygen contains 40.67% of carbon and 8.47% of hydrogen 0.5 g of that compound gives 94.91 mL of nitrogen at STP. What is the empirical formula of that compound?

(a) C_5H_2NO
(b) C_2H_5NO
(c) CHN_2O_5
(d) C_2HNO_5

10. Match the compounds given in Column I with the ratio of constituents (by mass) given in Column II and choose the correct answer using the codes given below the columns.

Column I	Column II
A. Water	1. 14 : 3
B. Ammonia	2. 1 : 8
C. Carbon dioxide	3. 1 : 1
D. Sulphur dioxide	4. 3 : 8

Codes

	A	B	C	D		A	B	C	D
(a)	1	2	4	3	(b)	2	1	4	3
(c)	2	1	3	4	(d)	4	1	3	2

11. 20.8 g of $BaCl_2$ on reaction with 9.8 g of H_2SO_4 produces 7.3 g of HCl and some amount of $BaSO_4$. The amount of $BaSO_4$ formed is

(a) 23.3 g (b) 20.8 g
(c) 9.8 g (d) 10.4 g

12. Which of the following reaction(s) is/are correct according to the law of conservation of mass?

I. $4Fe(s) + 3O_2(g) \longrightarrow 2Fe_2O_3(s)$

II. $2Mg(s) + O_2(g) \longrightarrow 2MgO(s)$

III. $P_4(s) + O_2(g) \longrightarrow P_4O_{10}(s)$

IV. $CH_4(g) + 2O_2(g) \longrightarrow CO_2(g) + 2H_2O(g)$

Codes

(a) Only I (b) I, II and IV
(c) II and III (d) III and IV

13. Shyam's teacher told him that the following data was obtained, when dinitrogen and dioxygen react together to form different compounds.

S.No.	Mass of dinitrogen	Mass of dioxygen
I	14 g	16 g
II	14 g	32 g
III	28 g	32 g
IV	28 g	80 g

Which law of chemical combination is obeyed by the above experimental data?
(a) Law of multiple proportions
(b) Law of conservation of mass
(c) Law of definite proportions
(d) All of the above

14. State [T] for True and [F] for False.
I. The symbol of silver is Si.
II. Noble gas molecules are diatomic.
III. Molecular mass of ethyne (C_2H_2) is 28 g/mol.
IV. The relative atomic mass of an element has no unit.

Codes

	I	II	III	IV		I	II	III	IV
(a)	T	F	F	T	(b)	F	T	T	F
(c)	F	F	F	T	(d)	F	T	F	F

15. Match the molecules given in Column I with their molecular mass given in Column II and choose the correct option using the codes given below the columns.

Column I	Column II
A. K_2CO_3	1. 62 u
B. Na_2O	2. 138 u
C. HNO_3	3. 64 u
D. SO_2	4. 63 u

Codes

	A	B	C	D		A	B	C	D
(a)	1	2	3	4	(b)	2	1	4	3
(c)	1	2	4	3	(d)	2	1	3	4

16. Aluminium sulphate is used in water purification and as a mordant in dyeing and printing textiles. In water purification, it causes impurities to coagulate into larger particles and then settle to the bottom of the container (or be filtered out more easily). This process is called coagulation or flocculation. The correct formula of aluminium sulphate is
(a) $AlSO_4$ (b) Al_2SO_4
(c) $Al_3(SO_4)_2$ (d) $Al_2(SO_4)_3$

17. Which of the following is/are not the penta-atomic ion?
I. Ammonium ion
II. Nitrate ion
III. Hydrogen carbonate ion
IV. Sulphate ion
V. Phosphate ion
VI. Sulphite ion

Codes
(a) I, II and VI (b) II, III and IV
(c) Only II (d) II and VI

18. Match the formula units given in Column I with their masses given in Column II and choose the correct answer using the codes given below the columns.

Column I	Column II
A. Calcium oxide	1. 56 u
B. Magnesium chloride	2. 95 u
C. Aluminium phosphide	3. 58 u
D. Calcium carbonate	4. 100 u

Codes

	A	B	C	D		A	B	C	D
(a)	1	3	2	4	(b)	1	2	3	4
(c)	1	3	4	2	(d)	3	1	4	2

19. Antacid are prescribed during acidity. Commercially available antacids consist of magnesium hydroxide [$Mg(OH)_2$], sugar and flavouring agents. The magnesium hydroxide act as base and form salt and water on reaction with hydrochloric acid of the stomach.

The mass of salt and water formed is equal to the combined mass of

(a) $Mg(OH)_2$ and HCl
(b) $Mg(OH)_2$, flavouring agent and HCl
(c) $Mg(OH)_2$, sugar and HCl
(d) $Mg(OH)_2$, sugar, flavouring agent and HCl

20. Match the formula units given in Column I with their masses given in Column II and choose the correct answer using the codes given below the columns.

Column I	Column II
A. Aluminium chloride	1. 100 u
B. Calcium carbonate	2. 133 u
C. Copper nitrate	3. 84 u
D. Sodium bicarbonate	4. 187.5 u

Codes

	A	B	C	D		A	B	C	D
(a)	1	2	3	4	(b)	2	4	1	3
(c)	2	1	4	3	(d)	1	2	4	3

21. State [T] for True and [F] for False.

I. Particles having more or less electrons than the normal atoms are called ions.
II. The molecular formula of a compound is determined by the valency of the elements present in the compound.
III. The molecular formula of ferrous sulphate is $Fe_2(SO_4)_3$ and ferric sulphate is $FeSO_4$.
IV. The formula of arsenic acid is H_3AsO_4. The name of its sodium salt, i.e. Na_3AsO_4 is sodium arsenate.

Codes

	I	II	III	IV
(a)	F	T	F	T
(b)	T	T	F	T
(c)	T	F	F	T
(d)	T	T	F	F

2 Marks Questions

22. Zinc sulphate contains 22.65% of zinc and 43.9% of water of crystallisation. If the law of constant proportions is true, then the weight of zinc required to produce 20 g of the crystals will be

(a) 45.3 g (b) 4.53 g
(c) 0.453 g (d) 453 g

23. **Statement I** When 10 g of $CaCO_3$ is decomposed, 5.6 g of residue is left and 4.4 g of CO_2 escapes.

Statement II An atom of aluminium is 27 times heavier than 1/12th of the mass of carbon-12.

Statement III In CO molecule, 12 parts by mass of carbon combine with 16 parts by mass of oxygen and in CO_2, 12 parts by mass of carbon combine with 32 parts by mass of oxygen.

Statement IV One atomic mass unit (amu) is mass of an atom equal to exactly. 1/12 times the ${}^{12}_{6}C$ isotope.

Which of the following statement(s) is/are correct.

(a) Only I (b) I and III
(c) II and III (d) All of these

24. Consider the preparation of three compounds A, B and C.

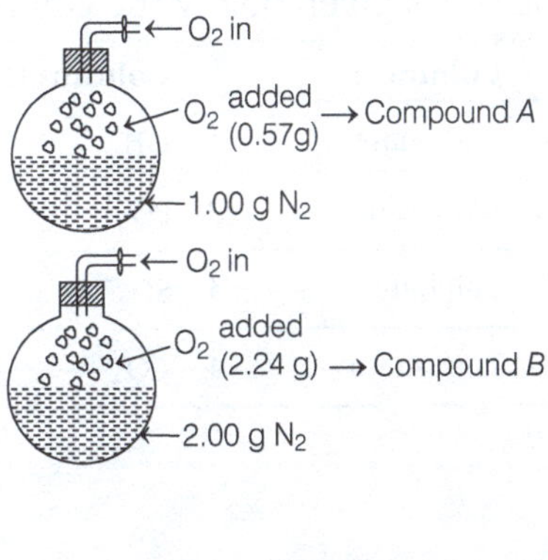

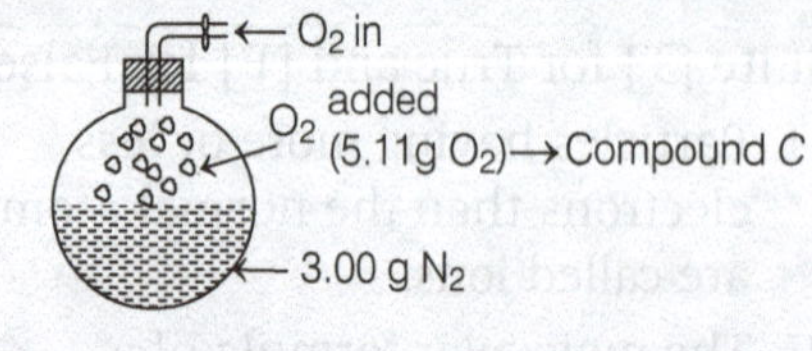

These above results obey which of the following laws?

(a) Law of constant proportions
(b) Law of multiple proportions
(c) Law of reciprocal proportions
(d) Law of partial pressures

25. In an experiment four substances are taken (in different moles) in separate close containers of equal dimensions and weight and they are weighed. The results in each case are given below.

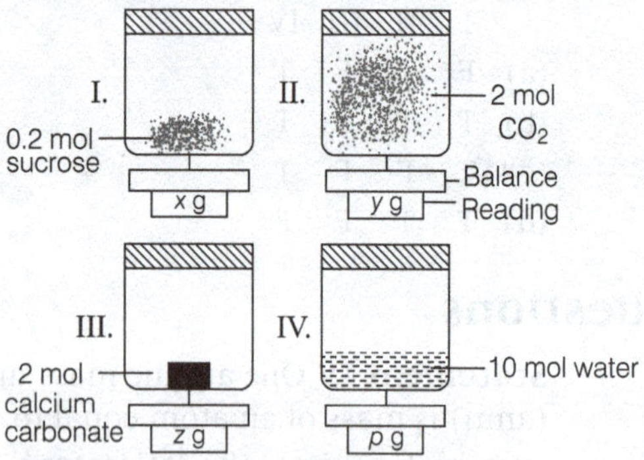

Which reading is the highest?

(a) x g (b) p g
(c) z g (d) y g

26. Match the ions given in Column I with their symbols given in Column II and choose the correct option using the codes given below the columns.

Column I	Column II
A. Carbonate	1. OH^-
B. Hydroxide	2. PO_4^{-3}
C. Sulphate	3. SO_4^{2-}
D. Phosphate	4. CO_3^{2-}

Codes

	A	B	C	D
(a)	1	2	3	4
(b)	4	1	3	2
(c)	1	4	2	3
(d)	4	3	2	1

27. Match the ions given in Column I with their symbols given in Column II and choose the correct option using the codes given below the columns.

Column I	Column II
A. Sulphite	1. HSO_3^-
B. Sulphide	2. SO_3^{2-}
C. Sulphate	3. S^{2-}
D. Bisulphite	4. SO_4^{2-}
	5. $S_2O_3^{2-}$

Codes

	A	B	C	D		A	B	C	D
(a)	5	1	4	3	(b)	3	1	4	5
(c)	2	3	4	1	(d)	2	3	1	4

28. Match the compounds given in Column I with the chemical formulae given in Column II and choose the correct answer using the codes given below the columns.

Column I	Column II
A. Carbon monoxide	1. MgS
B. Hydrogen chloride	2. AlF_3
C. Aluminium fluoride	3. HCl
D. Magnesium sulphide	4. CO

Codes

	A	B	C	D		A	B	C	D
(a)	4	3	2	1	(b)	3	4	1	2
(c)	4	3	1	2	(d)	3	1	4	2

Chapter

04

Structure of the Atom

1 Mark Questions

1. Consider the following information.

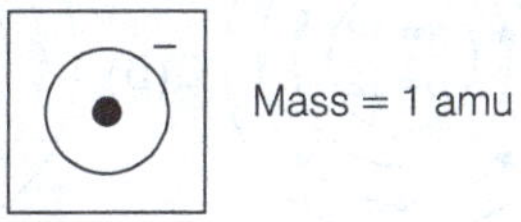

Ramana wants to neutralise it but the available particles for her are neutron, electron, proton and helium nuclei. Which will be the best species to fulfil the Ramana's need?

(a) A neutron (b) A proton
(c) An electron (d) A helium nucleus

2. Consider the following model of atom.

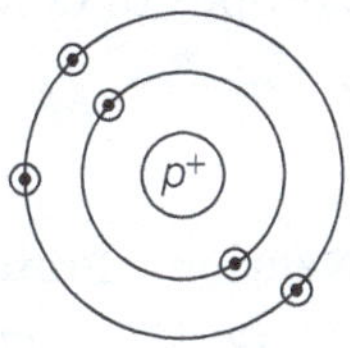

The experiment which established the above model of the atom, used a beam of

(a) β-particles which impinged on the metal foil and got absorbed
(b) γ-rays which impinged on a metal foil and ejected electrons
(c) hydrogen atoms, which impinged on a metal foil and got scattered
(d) helium nuclei, which impinged on a metal foil and got scattered

3. An atomic model is shown below.

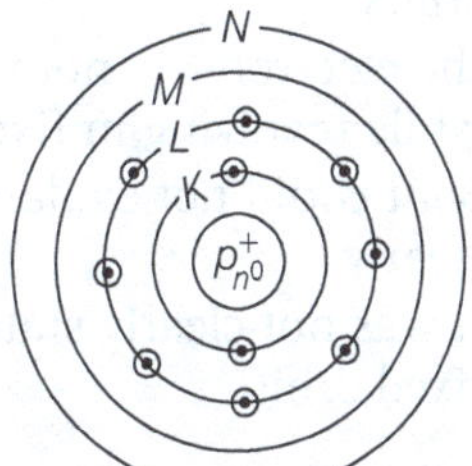

Which of the following statements does not form part of this model of atom?

(a) Energy of the electrons in the orbit is quantised
(b) The electron in the orbit nearest to the nucleus has the lowest energy
(c) Electrons revolve in different orbits around the nucleus
(d) The position and velocity of the electrons in the orbit cannot be determined simultaneously

4. Juan blew up a balloon. He then rubbed his hair with the balloon. When the balloon was moved away from his head, some of his hair stuck to the balloon. This is due to electrostatic attraction.

Which combination of charges could result in this attraction?

After being rubbed

	Hair	Balloon
(a)	Negatively charged	No charge
(b)	Positively charged	Negatively charged
(c)	No charge	Positively charged
(d)	Positively charged	Positively charged

5. In order to explain the stability of an atom, Niels Bohr gave a new arrangement of electrons in the atom that was based on the concept that

(a) the electrons could revolve around the nucleus in only certain fixed orbits

(b) the electrons do not radiate energy while revolving in fixed orbits

(c) Bohr could not explain the stability clearly

(d) it was not clearly stated about the fixed orbits

6. The diagram represents an atom of an element.

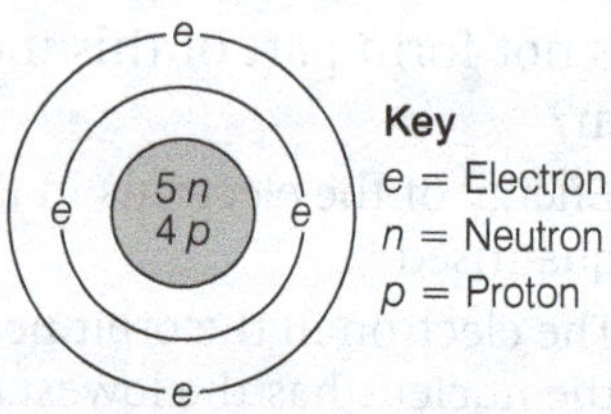

Which symbol gives this information?

(a) $^{9}_{4}Be$ (b) $^{9}_{5}B$

(c) $^{4}_{9}F$ (d) $^{13}_{8}O$

7. Which of the following figures do not represent Bohr's model of an atom correctly?

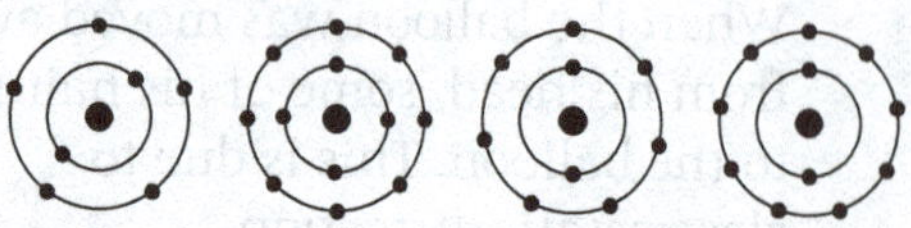

I II III IV

(a) I and II (b) II and III

(c) II and IV (d) I and IV

8. An element X is converted into its positive ion as $X \longrightarrow X^{3+}$.
Mass number of the atom is 27 and the number of neutrons is 14. What is the number of electrons in the ion?

(a) 13 (b) 10

(c) 14 (d) 16

9. Identify the Mg^{2+} ion from the figure where, n and p represent the number of neutrons and protons respectively.

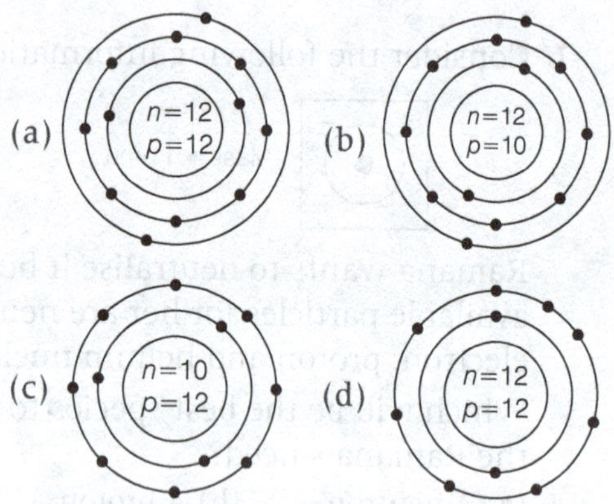

10. Which entry in the table shows the number of protons and neutrons in the two isotopes of chlorine $^{35}_{17}Cl$ and $^{37}_{17}Cl$?

	^{35}Cl		^{37}Cl	
	Protons	**Neutrons**	**Protons**	**Neutrons**
(a)	35	17	37	17
(b)	18	35	20	37
(c)	17	35	17	37
(d)	17	18	17	20

11. The relative atomic mass of naturally occurring chlorine is not a whole number.
What is the reason for this?

(a) Different chlorine atoms may have different numbers of neutrons

(b) Chlorine is unstable
(c) Naturally occurring chlorine cannot be obtained pure
(d) The mass of the electrons has been included

12. Choose the arrangement which shows the increasing value of *e/m* for e, p, n and α-particles.
(a) $n < \alpha < p < e$ (b) $e < p < \alpha < n$
(c) $n < p < e < \alpha$ (d) $p < n < \alpha < e$

13. Match the subatomic particles given in Column I with their discoverer given in Column II and choose the correct option using the codes given below:

	Column I		Column II
A.	Proton	1.	Thomson
B.	Electron	2.	Goldstein
C.	Neutron	3.	Anderson
D.	Positron	4.	Chadwick

Codes

	A	B	C	D		A	B	C	D
(a)	2	1	4	3	(b)	3	1	4	2
(c)	3	4	1	2	(d)	2	4	1	3

14. **Statement I** Cathode rays get deflected towards the positive plate of electric plate.
Statement II An ion has equal number of electrons and protons.
Which of the following statement(s) is/are correct?
(a) Only I (b) Only II
(c) Both I and II (d) Neither I nor II

15. The charge to mass ratio for a particle of the cathode rays was found to be 1.76×10^{11} C/kg. Comparing this value of *e/m* with that of H^+ ion showed that
(a) *e/m* value for the cathode ray particle was found to be 2000 times lesser than that for the H^+ ion
(b) the charge on the particle of the cathode ray is 2000 times larger than that on the H^+ ion
(c) the cathode ray particle is 2000 times smaller in mass than the H-atom
(d) Both (b) and (c) are correct

16. Atomic models have been improved over the years. Arrange the following atomic models in the order of their chronological order.
I. Rutherford's atomic model
II. Thomson's atomic model
III. Bohr's atomic model
Codes
(a) I, II and III
(b) II, III and I
(c) II, I and III
(d) III, II and I

17. In the Thomson's model of atom, which of the following statements are correct?
I. The mass of the atom is assumed to be uniformly distributed over the atom.
II. The positive charge is assumed to be uniformly distributed over the atom.
III. The electrons are uniformly distributed in the positively charged sphere.
IV. The electrons attract each other to stabilise the atom.
Codes
(a) I, II and III
(b) I and III
(c) I and IV
(d) I, III and IV

18. Match the Column I with Column II.

Column I	Column II
A. Dalton	1. Indivisibility of atoms
B. Niels Bohr	2. Discovery of electrons
C. Goldstein	3. Stationary orbits
D. Rutherford	4. Canal rays
	5. Concept of nucleus

Codes

	A	B	C	D		A	B	C	D
(a)	1	3	4	5	(b)	1	3	2	4
(c)	4	2	1	3	(d)	5	2	3	1

19. Which of the following statements about Rutherford's model of atom is/are correct?

I. Considered the nucleus as positively charged.

II. Established that the α-particles are four times as heavy as a hydrogen atom.

III. Can be compared to solar system.

IV. Was in agreement with Thomson's model.

Codes

(a) I and III (b) II and III
(c) I and IV (d) Only I

20. The atoms of element *Y* have the electronic configuration 2, 8, 6.

Which statement about element *Y* is correct?

I. It forms an ionic compound with sodium.

II. It forms an ion with a charge of 2+.

III. It has 6 protons in the outer shell of an atom.

IV. It only reacts with non-metals.

Codes

(a) I and III (b) I, III and IV
(c) Only I (d) II, III and IV

21. Consider the following table.

Mass number	Atomic number	Electronic configuration				Number of valence electrons
		K	*L*	*M*	*N*	
12	6	2	*Y*	—		4
40	20	*X*	8	8	*Z*	2

The values of *X*, *Y* and *Z*, respectively are

(a) 2, 2, 2 (b) 2, 4, 2
(c) 0, 4, 2 (d) 0, 8, 2

22. In which set do the three particles each have the same total number of electrons?

I. Cl^-, Br^-, I^-

II. F^-, Ne, Na^+

III. K^+, Ca^{2+}, Br^-

IV. Li^+, Na^+, K^+

The correct answer is

(a) I, II and III
(b) II, III and IV
(c) II and III
(d) Only II

23. The elements *A*, *B* and *C* have following composition.

Element	Protons	Neutrons	Electrons
A	8	8	8
B	8	9	8
C	8	10	8

The species have

(a) same physical and chemical properties
(b) same physical properties but different chemical properties
(c) same chemical properties but different physical properties
(d) different physical and chemical properties

24. Some triads of nuclei, which may be isotones, are given below.

I. ${}_6C^{14}, {}_7N^{15}, {}_9F^{17}$

II. ${}_6C^{12}, {}_7N^{14}, {}_9F^{19}$

III. ${}_6C^{14}, {}_7N^{14}, {}_9F^{17}$

IV. ${}_6C^{14}, {}_7N^{14}, {}_9F^{19}$

The correct set which represents isotones is

(a) I and II
(b) II and III
(c) Only I
(d) All of the above

25. Match the entries of Column I with appropriate entries of Column II.

Column I	Column II
A. Isotopes	1. ${}^{40}_{18}Ar$, ${}^{40}_{19}K$, ${}^{40}_{20}Ca$
B. Isobars	2. ${}^{16}_{8}O$, ${}^{17}_{8}O$, ${}^{18}_{8}O$
C. Isotones	3. O^{2-}, Na^{+}, Mg^{2+}
D. Isoelectronics	4. ${}^{14}_{6}C$, ${}^{15}_{7}N$, ${}^{16}_{8}O$

Codes

	A	B	C	D
(a)	2	1	4	3
(b)	3	2	4	1
(c)	4	1	2	3
(d)	2	3	1	4

2 Marks Questions

26. State [T] for True and [F] for False.

I. J.J. Thomson proposed that the nucleus of an atom contains only neutrons.

II. Rutherford concluded from the α-particles scattering experiment that positive charge of an atom occupies maximum space.

III. Rutherford's α-particle scattering experiment led to the discovery of nucleus.

IV. As we move away from the nucleus, the energy of orbit decreases.

V. Thomson assumed atom as a pudding of electrons in which positive charge (raisins) are embedded.

VI. The radius of nucleus of an atom is 10^{-15} m and the radius of an atom is 10^{-10} m.

Codes

	I	II	III	IV	V	VI
(a)	T	T	F	F	T	T
(b)	F	F	T	T	F	F
(c)	F	F	T	F	F	T
(d)	F	T	F	T	F	T

27. State [T] for True and [F] for False.

I. The innermost atomic shell can held a maximum of 18 electrons.

II. The number of protons in Na^{+} is 10. It means that, it contains more electrons as compared to protons.

III. Number of valence electrons in chloride ion is 8.

IV. A particular element has electronic configuration 2, 7. In reactions, it forms compounds by loss of one electron.

V. The electrons present in the *M* shell of an atom of an element with atomic number 24 is 13.

VI. Elements with valency 1 are always metals.

Codes

	I	II	III	IV	V	VI
(a)	T	F	T	F	T	T
(b)	F	F	T	F	T	T
(c)	T	T	F	T	T	F
(d)	F	F	T	F	T	F

28. If bromine atom is available in the form of, say, two isotopes $^{79}_{35}Br$ (49.7%) and $^{81}_{35}Br$ (50.3%), the average atomic mass of bromine atom is

(a) 81 (b) 80
(c) 79 (d) 80.5

29. State [T] for True and [F] for False.

I. An isotope of iodine is used for making tincture of iodine, which is used as a medicine.

II. Isobars because of the presence of same number of nucleons have same chemical properties.

III. Isotones are the species in which difference between the total number of nucleons and total number of protons is the same.

IV. Atomic mass of chlorine is fractional because it exists in several isotopic forms.

V. An isotope of cobalt (Co-60) is used to detect blood clot.

VI. Isobars shares their electronic configuration, i.e. have same electronic configuration but isotopes do not.

Codes

	I	II	III	IV	V	VI
(a)	F	F	T	T	F	F
(b)	F	F	F	T	T	T
(c)	F	T	T	F	T	F
(d)	F	T	F	T	F	T

30. A beam of particles contains neutrons (n), protons (p) and electrons (e). The beam is passed between charged plates.

Which diagrams shows how the particles are affected by the plates?

I.
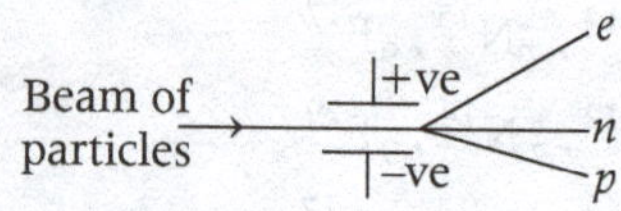

II.
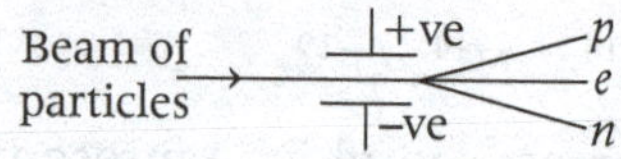

III.
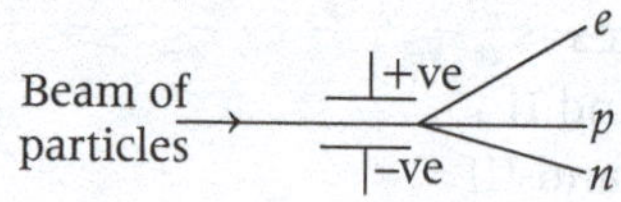

IV.
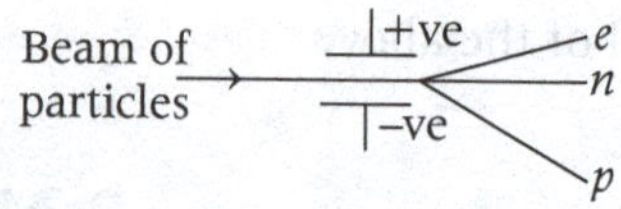

Codes

(a) Only I
(b) I and IV
(c) III and IV
(d) I and II

31. An element X has two isotopes, which may be represented as ^{238}X and ^{235}X. How does ^{238}X differ from ^{235}X?

(a) It has 3 more protons and 3 more electrons
(b) It has 3 more protons but no more electrons
(c) It has 3 more neutrons and 3 more electrons
(d) It has 3 more neutrons but no more electrons

32. Vanadium is a transition element. Its atomic number and mass number are respectively 92 and 235. The ratio of neutron to proton in this element is

(a) 1.52 (b) 1.33
(c) 1.55 (d) 1.42

Chapter
05

The Fundamental Unit of Life

1 Mark Questions

1. Rahim's teacher wrote the following statements about an organism *A*.

I. Organism *A* is a plant.
II. Organism *A* feeds on other organisms.
III. Organism *A* needs energy to stay alive.
IV. Organism *A* can be seen with naked eye.

Which of the following statements can Rahim use to conclude that organism *A* is made up of many cells?

(a) Only III (b) II and III
(c) I and IV (d) I, II, III and IV

2. Observe the given cells *X*, *Y* and *Z*.

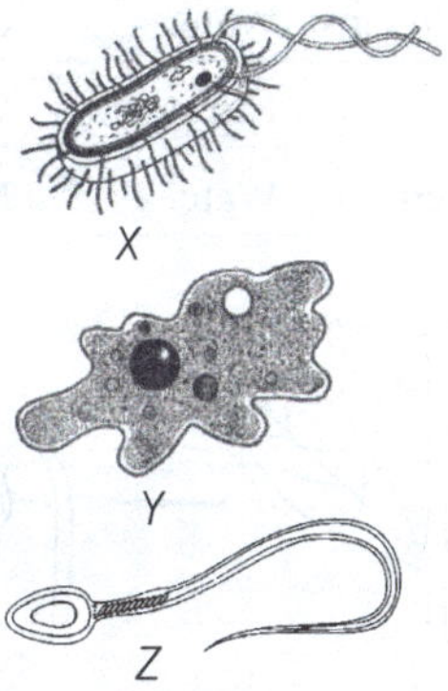

Name all these cells and differentiate into eukaryotic and prokaryotic cells.

	Eukaryotic	Prokaryotic
(a)	*X*–Fungal, *Y*–Neuron cell	*Z*–*Paramecium*
(b)	*X*–Algal cell	*Y*–Bone cell, *Z*–*Euglena*
(c)	*Z*–Sperm, *Y*–*Amoeba*	*X*–Bacterial cell
(d)	*X*–Bacterial cell *Z*–Bone marrow cell	*Y*–Blood cell

3. Match the Column I with Column II.

Column I	Column II
A. Robert Hooke	1. Discovery of nucleus
B. Schleiden and Schwann	2. Protoplasm
C. Robert Brown	3. Cell theory
D. Purkinje	4. Discovered cell

Codes

	A	B	C	D
(a)	4	3	2	1
(b)	3	4	1	2
(c)	4	3	1	2
(d)	1	2	3	4

4. The diagram shows a root hair cell. Which structure controls the uptake of nitrate ions into the cell?

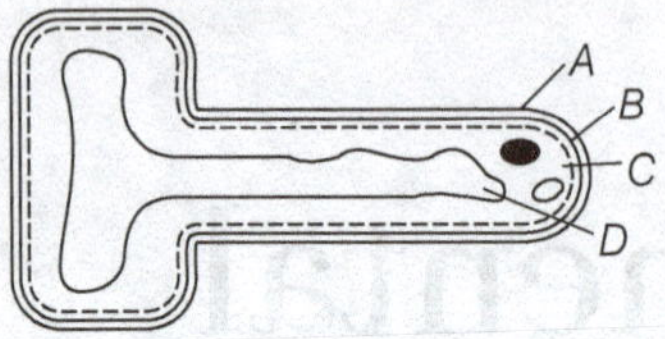

(a) *A* (b) *B* (c) *C* (d) *D*

5. The diagram shows four types of cell, not drawn to scale.

Which cell does not contain cytoplasm?

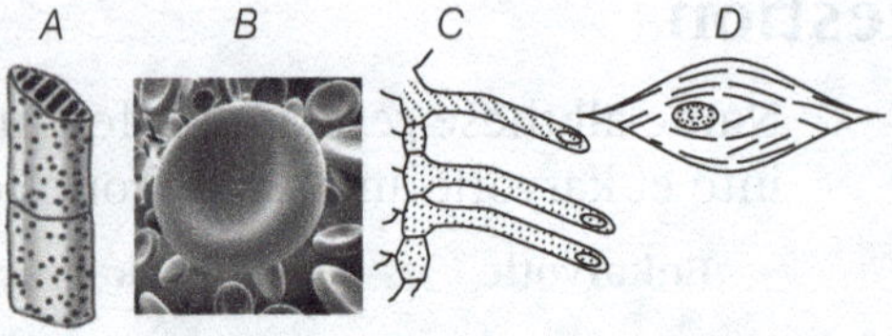

(a) *A* (b) *B* (c) *C* (d) *D*

6. The diagram given below shows the longitudinal section of collenchyma tissue.

Label the parts *A*, *B*, *C* and *D* in the given diagram.

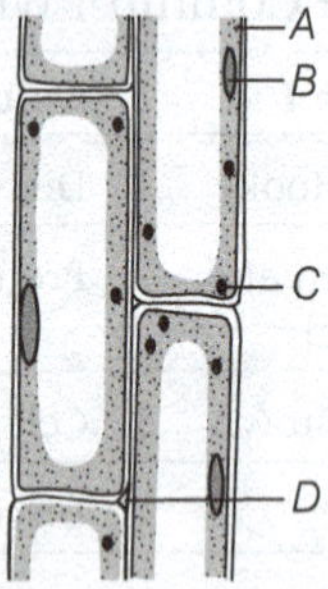

	A	*B*	*C*	*D*
(a)	Intercellular space	Nucleus	Chloroplast	Cytoplasm
(b)	Chloroplast	Nucleus	Intercellular space	Cytoplasm
(c)	Cytoplasm	Intercellular space	Nucleus	Chloroplast
(d)	Cytoplasm	Nucleus	Chloroplast	Intercellular space

7. A lysosome is a tiny, single membranous vesicle but contains powerful digestive enzymes that are capable of breaking down the organic material. Suppose these vesicles burst inside the cell, what will be the resultant effect of it on the cell?

(a) Only the nearby organelles will effect

(b) Cytoplasm contain plenty of water, thus there will be no effect on cell

(c) Whole cell will be digested or will die

(d) It will show no effect

8.

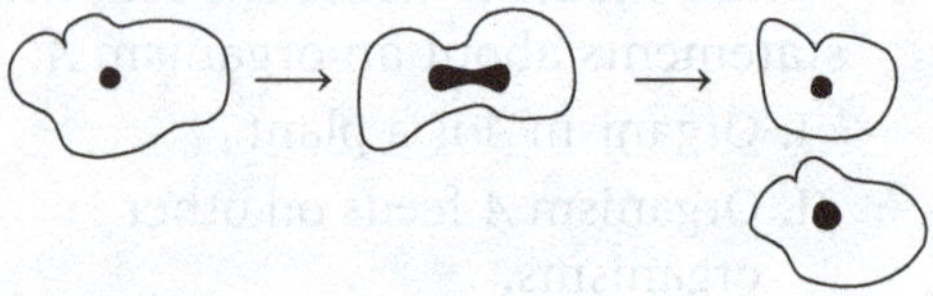

The above diagram says

(a) All animals are made up of cells

(b) All plants are made up of cells

(c) Cell is the basic functional unit of life

(d) All cells arise from pre-existing cells

9. How do nitrate ions, oxygen and water enter root hair cells?

	By active transport	By diffusion	By osmosis
(a)	Nitrate ions	Oxygen	Water
(b)	Nitrate ions	Water	Oxygen
(c)	Oxygen	Nitrate ions	Water
(d)	Oxygen	Water	Nitrate ions

10.

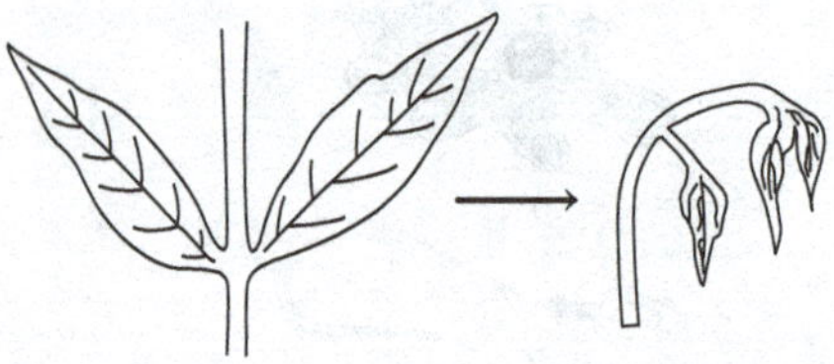

What is the phenomenon illustrated in the diagram?
(a) Collapse of the xylem
(b) Plasmolysis
(c) Translocation
(d) Wilting

11. Two beakers *A* and *B* are taken. Beaker *A* is filled with normal water and beaker *B* is filled with a concentrated sugar solution.
A few raisins are put in both the beakers. What will happen to the raisins put in beakers *A* and *B*, respectively? Select the right observation.

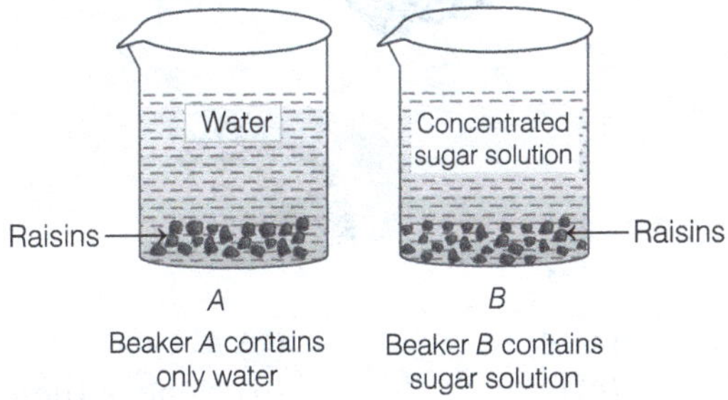

(a) Raisins in beaker *A* swells up due to the endosmosis and raisins in beaker *B* shrinks due to the exosmosis
(b) Raisins in beaker *A* shrinks due to the exosmosis and raisins in beaker *B* swells up due to the endosmosis
(c) Raisins in beaker *A* swells up due to the exosmosis and raisins in beaker *B* shrinks due to the endosmosis
(d) In both beakers *A* and *B*, endosmosis will occur

12. Two solutions of different concentrations (*A* and *B*) are separated by means of a membrane (*C*). Which of the following option is correct (take X = solute and Y = water)?

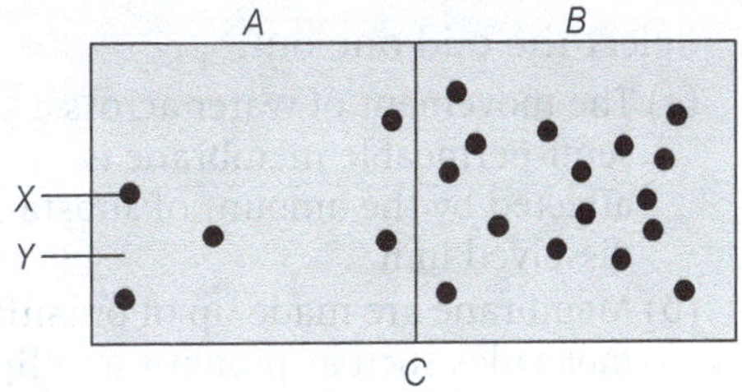

	Nature of membrane (*R*)	Net movement	Direction of movement
(a)	Permeable	X	A → B
(b)	Permeable	Y	A → B
(c)	Semipermeable	Y	B → A
(d)	Semipermeable	Y	A → B

13. Which structures are present in animal cells?

	Cell membrane	Cell wall	Chloroplast	Cytoplasm
(a)	7	3	3	3
(b)	3	7	7	3
(c)	3	7	3	7
(d)	3	3	7	3

14. A human red blood cell is placed in a strong salt solution.
In which direction does water move and what is the effect on the cell?

	Movement of water	Effect on cell
(a)	Into the cell	Slight increase in size
(b)	Into the cell	Cell bursts
(c)	Out of the cell	Cell shrinks
(d)	Out of the cell	No change in cell volume

15. Consider the following statement and choose the correct option. The plasma membrane control the loss and will leave the cell with the help of various process, e.g. osmosis, diffusion, imbibition, etc.

Select the odd one out.
(a) The movement of water across a semi-permeable membrane is affected by the amount of substances dissolved in it
(b) Membrane are made up of organic molecules such as proteins and lipids
(c) Molecules soluble in organic solvents can easily pass through the membrane
(d) Plasma membrane contain chitin sugar in plants

16. Match the Column I with Column II.

Column I	Column II
A. Cell	1. Leaf
B. Organ	2. Heart
C. Tissue	3. Skeleton
D. Organ system	4. Root hair
E. Organism	5. Spongy mesophyll
	6. Worm
	7. Kidney
	8. Xylem

Codes

	A	B	C	D	E
(a)	5	1, 2, 7	4, 8	3	6
(b)	3	2, 7	1, 6	4	5, 8
(c)	1	2, 6	3, 7	4	5, 8
(d)	8	7, 1	3, 6	5	4, 2

17. Refer to the given Venn diagram and choose the correct option.

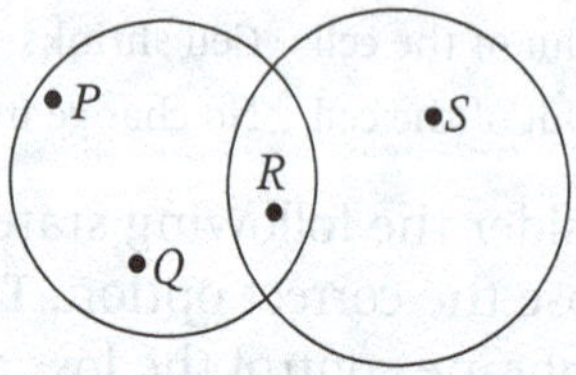

Plant cell Animal cell

	P	Q	R	S
(a)	Cell membrane	Cytoplasm	Nucleus	Mitochondria
(b)	Cell wall	Chloroplast	Cell membrane	Centriole
(c)	Plastid	Cytoplasm	Cell wall	Nucleus
(d)	Nucleus	Cell wall	Cytoplasm	Cell membrane

18. There are three cell organelles as given below. Observe them and select which cell organelle contains both DNA and ribosome.

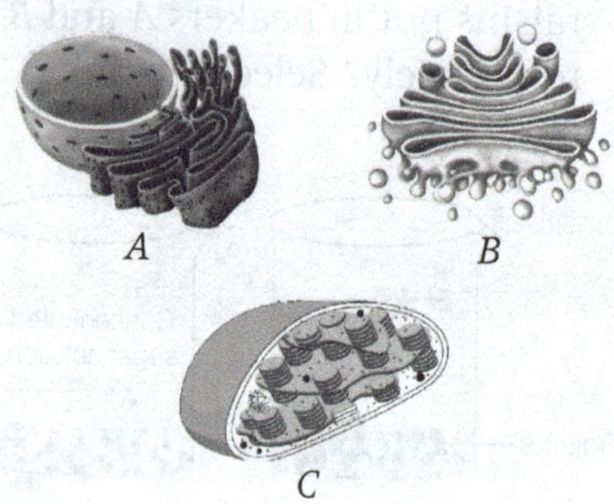

(a) *A* (b) *B*
(c) *C* (d) None of these

19. State (T) for True and (F) for False.
I. Cell wall of prokaryotic cell is made up of cellulose, chitin and hemicellulose.
II. Spindle fibres are present in prokaryotic cells.
III. Prokaryotic cell have 80S ribosomes.
IV. Flagella have 9-12 arrangement in eukaryotic cells.

Codes

	I	II	III	IV
(a)	T	T	F	T
(b)	F	T	T	T
(c)	T	T	T	T
(d)	F	F	F	F

20. **Assertion** (A) Plasma membrane is called a selectively permeable membrane.

Reason (R) CO_2 and O_2 moves in and out of cell through diffusion.

(a) Both A and R are true and R is the correct explanation of A
(b) Both A and R are true, but R is not the correct explanation of A
(c) A is true, but R is false
(d) A is false, but R is true

21. Plants use CO_2 to form glucose as their food and release O_2 in environment. This process is termed as photosynthesis. This process generally takes part in chloroplast of the plant cell. In which part of the chloroplast, this process takes place?

(a) Outer membrane and inner membrane
(b) Lamella and intermembrane space
(c) Granum and stroma
(d) Thylakoid and lumen

22. Which of the following cell organelle take part in the formation of acrosome?

(a) Nucleus (b) Chromosome
(c) Golgi complex (d) Mitochondria

23. Which one of the given options is not true?

I. Mitochondria is involved in the formation of lysosomes.
II. Nucleus, mitochondria and chloroplast have DNA. Hence, they are able to make their own protein.
III. Mitochondria is said to be the powerhouse of the cell as ATP is generated in them.
IV. Cytoplasm is called as protoplasm.

Codes

(a) I and IV
(b) III and IV
(c) I and II
(d) II and IV

24. In which of the following endoplasmic reticulum is absent?

(a) Cell of pancreas and salivary gland
(b) Erythrocytes of mammals and prokaryotes
(c) Cell of brain
(d) Nephrons

2 Marks Questions

25. Three fresh vegetables, i.e. potato, tomato and spinach are taken for an experiment.

The experiment was to obtain plastids from all these vegetables. Which plastid will obtain from all these vegetables? Select the correct option.

	Potato	Tomato	Spinach
(a)	Chromoplast	Leucoplast	Chloroplast
(b)	Chromoplast	Chloroplast	Leucoplast
(c)	Leucoplast	Chromoplast	Chloroplast
(d)	Chloroplast	Leucoplast	Chromoplast

26. Which among the following cells is involved in continuity of life?

(a) 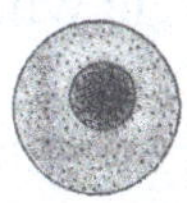
(b) 
(c) 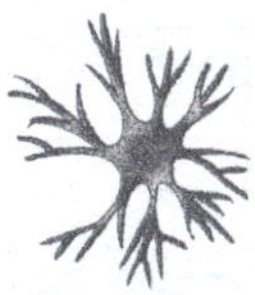
(d) 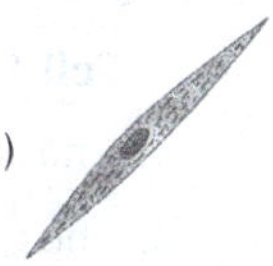

27. Refer to the given diagram related to osmosis and choose the correct option.

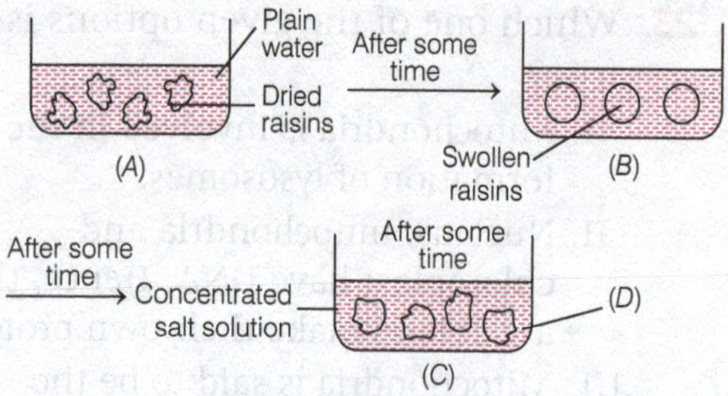

	A	*B*	*C*	*D*
(a)	Shrunken raisins	Endosmosis	Exosmosis	Dried raisins
(b)	Dried raisins	Exosmosis	Endosmosis	Shrunken raisins
(c)	Dried raisins	Endosmosis	Exosmosis	Shrunken raisins
(d)	Shrunken raisins	Exosmosis	Endosmosis	Dried raisins

28.

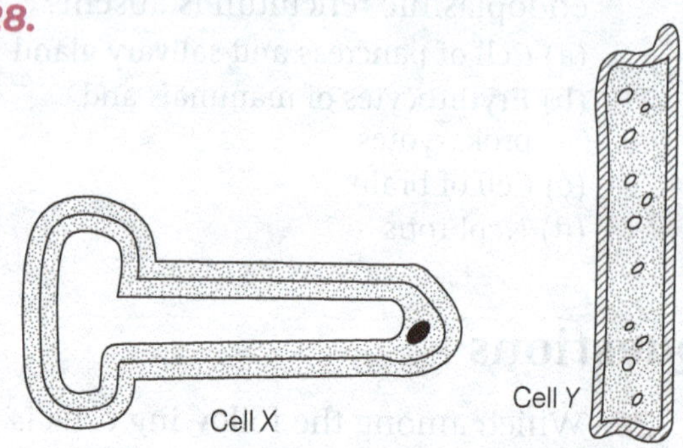

The diagram shows two plant cells. These cells become turgid when they take up water by osmosis.
In which of these cells does, being turgid provide support?

	Cell *X*	Cell *Y*
A	no	no
B	no	yes
C	yes	no
D	yes	yes

(a) A (b) B (c) C (d) D

29. The given diagram shows the process of

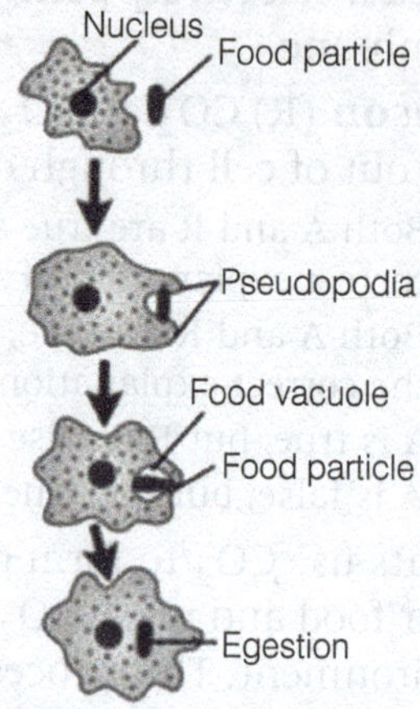

(a) endosmosis (b) phagocytosis
(c) exosmosis (d) pinocytosis

30. Which one of the given options is true?

I. Cytoplasm is general mass of protoplasm excluding nucleus.
II. Nucleoplasm contains nucleolus, chromosomes, etc.
III. Cytoplasm is a semi-fluid ground substance found in nucleus.
IV. Cytoplasm contains the organelles, vitamins, enzymes and sugars, etc.

Codes

(a) Only I (b) I, II and IV
(c) II, III and IV (d) II and IV

31. The given diagram shows the cross-section of a single cell.

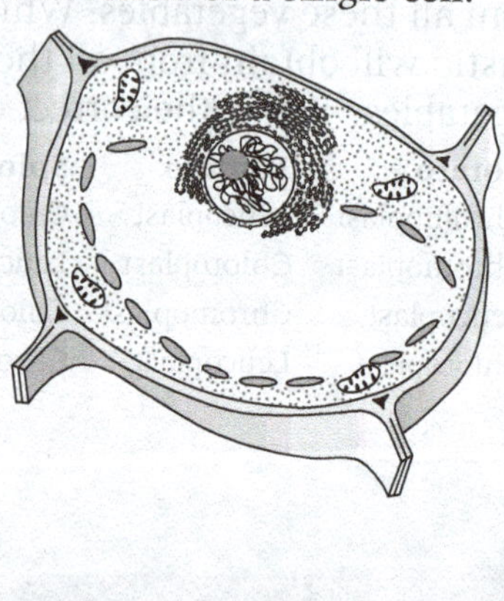

A student is convinced that the above cell is an animal cell. Which of the following evidence would you use to convince him otherwise?

I. The cell has a cell wall.

II. The cell appears to be able to carry out photosynthesis.

III. The cell has only one visible vacuole.

IV. The cell has numerous mitochondria.

(a) Only I
(b) I and II
(c) I, II and III
(d) I, II, III and IV

32. Consider the following statements.

Cellular organisms are divided into two main types as prokaryotes and eukaryotes. In prokaryotic cells, membrane bound organelles are absent whereas in eukaryotic cells they are present.

A. They are not considered as part of the endomembrane system.

B. Double membrane bound organelles.

C. Both have 70S ribosome.

Choose the correct option with respect to A, B and C.

These characters are shown by the organelles

(a) Lysosomes and SER
(b) RER and Golgi apparatus
(c) Chloroplast and mitochondria
(d) Peroxisomes and mitochondria

33. Which visible features of the plant cell in the diagram distinguishes it from an animal cell?

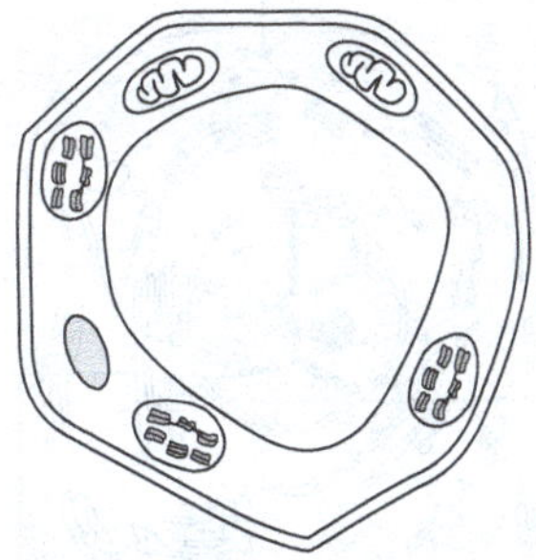

I. Absence of numerous small vacuoles.

II. Cytoplasm pushed to periphery of the cell.

III. Presence of chloroplasts.

IV. Presence of cell wall.

Codes

(a) Only IV
(b) III and IV
(c) I, III and IV
(d) II, III and IV

34. Organelle *X* is involved in the formation of organelle *Y*, which is also known as 'suicidal bags' of the cell. Organelle *X* has cisternae and enzymes of organelle *Y* are made by organelle *Z*.

Choose the correct option for *X*, *Y* and *Z*.

	X	*Y*	*Z*
(a)	Mitochondria	Lysosomes	Golgi body
(b)	Golgi body	Mitochondria	Lysosomes
(c)	Golgi body	Lysosomes	RER
(d)	RER	Lysosomes	Golgi body

35. The diagram below shows some of the structures in an animal cell.

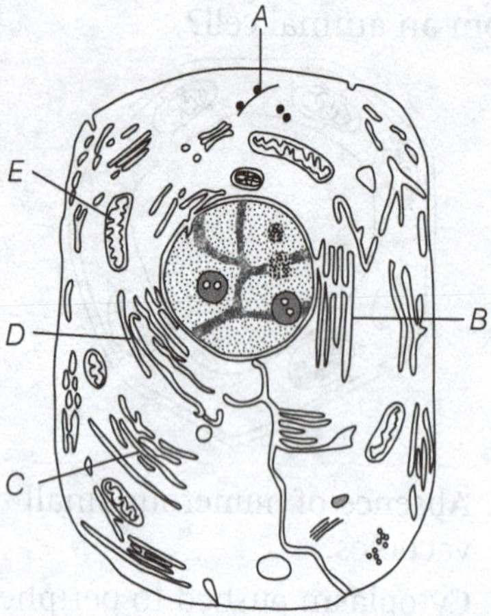

Which one of the following structures *A*, *B*, *C*, *D* and *E* would be involved in the final secretion of digestive enzymes from this cell?

(a) '*A*' marked organelle
(b) '*B*' marked organelle
(c) '*D*' and '*E*' marked organelles
(d) '*C*' marked organelle

36.

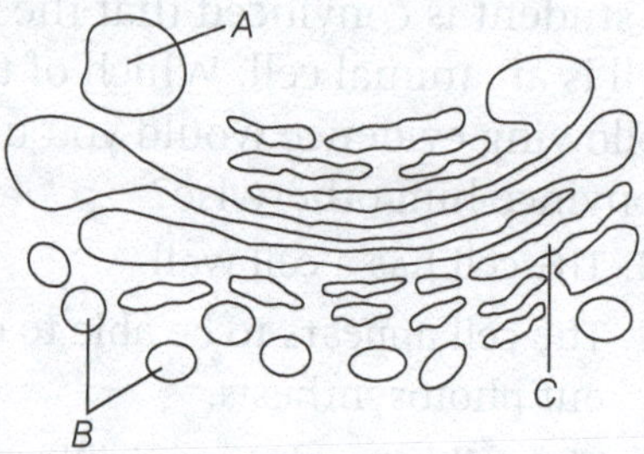

Identify the labels *A*, *B* and *C* of Golgi apparatus.

(a) *A*–Vacuole, *B*–Secretory vesicle, *C*–Cisternae
(b) *A*–Secretory vesicle, *B*–Vacuole, *C*–Cisternae
(c) *A*–Cisternae, *B*-Vacuole, *C*–Secretory vesicle
(d) None of the above

37. Plastids present in most plant cells and are absent in animal cells. Like mitochondria, plastids also have their own genome (i.e. DNA) and ribosomes. They are self-replicating organelles. Plastids are of three types.

Name of the plastids	Colour of the pigment present	Functions	Location
Chloroplast	Green (chlorophyll)	Involved in photosynthesis	Leaves
Chromoplast	*B*	Imparts attractive colours to the plants	Coloured parts of the plants
A	Colourless	Stores starch, oils and protein granules	Non-photosynthetic tissues of plants, such as roots, bulbs and seeds.

From the table above identify *A* and *B*.

(a) *A*–Leucoplast and *B*-Any color
(b) *A*–Elaioplast and *B*-Purple
(c) *A*–Leucoplast and *B*-Any colour (except green)
(d) None of the above

38. Match the Column I with Column II.

	Column I		Column II
A.	Cell wall	1.	Head quarter of the cell
B.	Nucleus	2.	Security guard of the cell
C.	Endoplasmic reticulum	3.	Kitchen of the cell
D.	Chloroplast	4.	Suicidal bags of the cell
E.	Golgi body	5.	Channel for transportation and detoxification
F.	Lysosome	6.	Packaging of product and formation of lysosome

Codes

	A	B	C	D	E	F
(a)	2	1	6	5	4	3
(b)	2	1	5	3	6	4
(c)	6	5	4	3	1	2
(d)	1	2	4	3	6	5

39. Which of the following is true about cell division?

I. Mitosis occurs in germ cells of the body of organisms.

II. Four daughter cells are formed as a result of meiosis.

III. In both meiosis and mitosis the number of chromosomes remains same.

IV. Meiosis is helpful in sexual reproduction by forming male and female gametes.

Codes

(a) I, II and IV (b) Only IV

(c) II and IV (d) I, II and III

Chapter 06

Tissues

1 Mark Questions

1. If the tip of sugarcane plant is removed from the field, even then it keeps on growing in length. Which part of the plant is responsible for this? Select the correct option.

(a) Cambium
(b) Apical meristem
(c) Lateral meristem
(d) Intercalary meristem

2. Refer to the Venn diagram and choose the correct option for *A*.

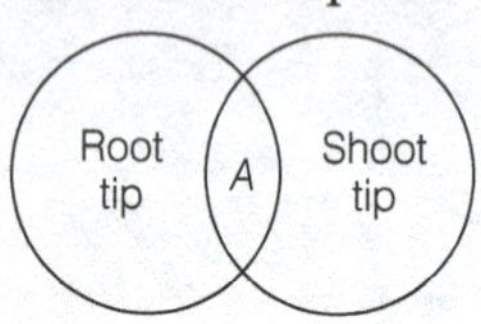

(a) Apical meristem
(b) Intercalary meristem
(c) Lateral meristem
(d) Both (b) and (c)

3. Two friends Ashley and Mary are playing in a park. There were two trees in the park. Tree *A* has wider trunk than tree *B*. Ashley and Mary argue as

Ashley Tree *B* is older than tree *A*.
Mary Tree *A* is older than Tree *B*.
Who made the correct statement?

(a) Ashley (b) Mary
(c) Both of them (d) None of these

4. Identify the labels in the given figure.

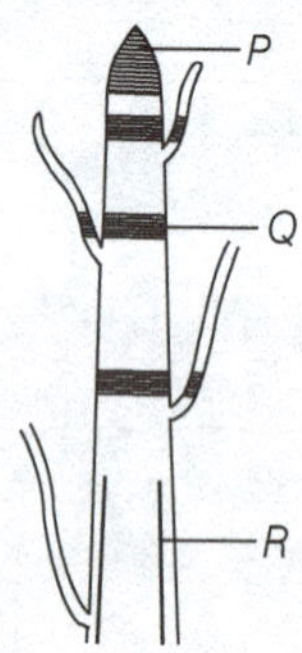

	P	*Q*	*R*
(a)	Intercalary meristem	Apical meristem	Lateral meristem
(b)	Apical meristem	Lateral meristem	Intercalary meristem
(c)	Apical meristem	Intercalary meristem	Lateral meristem
(d)	Lateral meristem	Apical meristem	Intercalary meristem

5. A microscopic view of a plant tissue is given below, observe it carefully and name *A*, *B* and *C* correctly.

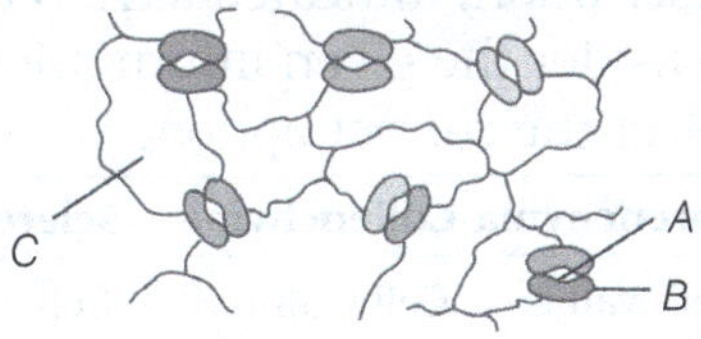

	A	*B*	*C*
(a)	Stomata	Guard cell	Epidermal cell
(b)	Guard cell	Stomata	Epidermal cell
(c)	Epidermal cell	Guard cell	Stomata
(d)	Stomata	Epidermal cell	Guard cell

6. The roots of onion stops to grow in jar 2 once we cut their tips because

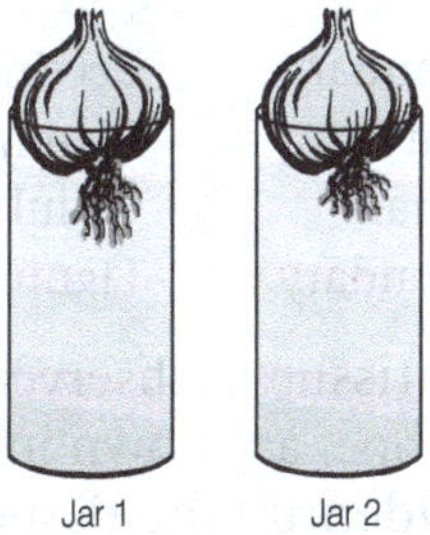

(a) the plant growth continue in other parts
(b) the meristematic growth is stopped
(c) the plant continues to grow laterally
(d) All of the above

7. Assertion (A) Intercalary meristem increases length of plant like apical meristem.

Reason (R) Intercalary meristem originates from the apical meristem.

(a) Both A and R are true and R is the correct explanation of A
(b) Both A and R are true, but R is not a correct explanation of A
(c) A is true, but R is false
(d) A is false, but R is true

8. Which of the following is true?

(a) Vessels are multicellular tube-like structures with wide lumen
(b) Tracheids are multicellular tube-like structures with wide broad ends
(c) Vessels are unicellular tube-like structures with wide lumen
(d) Tracheids are unicellular tube-like structures with wide lumen

9. Assertion (A) Xylem is a complex tissue.

Reason (R) Xylem and phloem constitute a vascular bundle.

(a) Both A and R are true and R is the correct explanation of A
(b) Both A and R are true, but R is not the correct explanation of A
(c) A is true, but R is false
(d) A is false, but R is true

10. A long tree has several branches. The tissue that helps in the lateral conduction of water in the branches is

(a) collenchyma
(b) xylem parenchyma
(c) parenchyma
(d) xylem vessels

11. Observe the figure given below and identify the parts labelled as *A*,*B* and *C*.

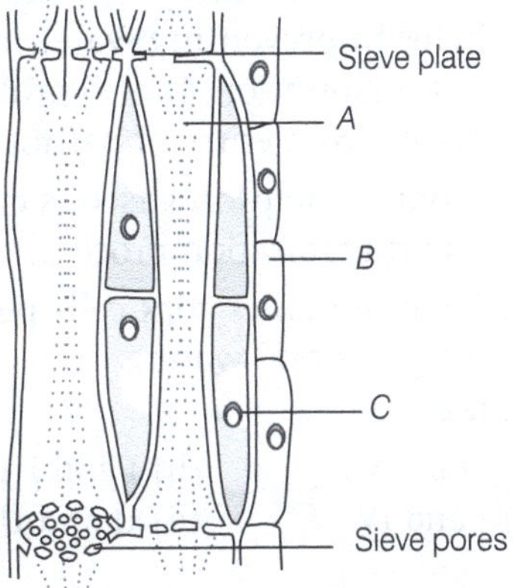

	A	*B*	*C*
(a)	Sieve tube	Companion cell	Phloem parenchyma
(b)	Sieve tube	Phloem parenchyma	Companion cell
(c)	Companion cell	Phloem parenchyma	Sieve tube
(d)	Phloem parenchyma	Companion cell	Sieve tube

12. Match the Column I with Column II.

Column I	Column II
A. Cambium	1. Air cavities
B. Phelloderm	2. Round nuclei
C. Columnar epithelium	3. Elongated nuclei
D. Cuboidal epithelium	4. Cork
E. Aerenchyma	5. Lateral meristem

Codes

	A	B	C	D	E
(a)	5	2	3	4	1
(b)	4	3	2	5	1
(c)	5	4	3	2	1
(d)	1	4	2	3	5

13. Select the incorrect statement(s).

I. Hair like structure called root hairs on epidermal cells reduce the total absorptive surface area.

II. Cutin has a waterproof quality and helps in preventing water loss due to transpiration. It also protects plants from entry of pathogens, etc.

III. Stomata helps in gaseous exchange and transpiration process.

IV. Suberin makes cork cells permeable for gases and water.

Codes

(a) Only IV (b) I and III
(c) I and IV (d) II and III

14. A few characteristic features of the three types of cells are given below. Some parts are missing in this description, indicated as *A*, *B* and *C*. Consider the given information and select the correct option.

Parenchyma	Collenchyma	Sclerenchyma
Cell wall is primary.	Cell wall is *A*.	Cell wall is secondary.
Cell wall is made up of cellulose.	Cell wall is made up of cellulose and pectin.	Cell wall is made up of *B*.
They are living cells.	They are *C* cells.	They are dead cells.

Codes

	A	*B*	*C*
(a)	Secondary	Pectin	Dead
(b)	Primary	Lignin	Living
(c)	Primary	Cellulose	Living
(d)	Secondary	Lignin	Dead

15. A plant tissue is observed under a microscope, as shown in the figure below. Identify the tissue. Name any one part of the plant, where such cells are present.

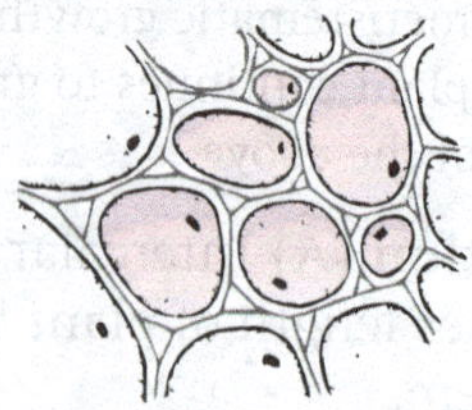

I. Collenchyma, pith.
II. Sclerenchyma, medullary rays.
III. Parenchyma, pith.
IV. Parenchyma, cortex.

Codes

(a) I and II (b) I and III
(c) III and IV (d) IV and II

16. The given diagram is of *A* tissue. This is a kind of animal tissue. It is found in the inner lining of *B*, *C*, *D* vessels and covering of tongue.

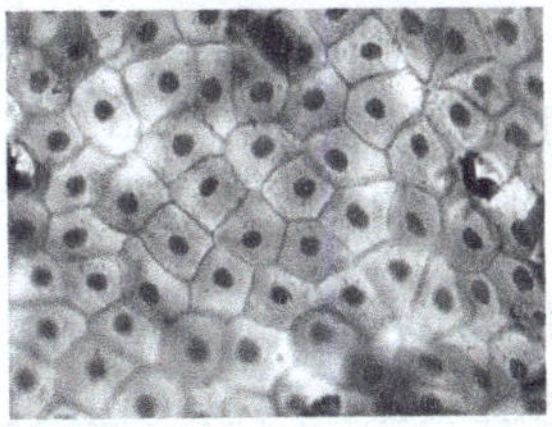

	A	*B*	*C*	*D*
(a)	Epithelial	Mouth	Oesophagus	Blood vessels
(b)	Tongue	Blood vessels	Oesophagus	Mouth
(c)	Muscular	Blood vessels	Mouth	Oesophagus
(d)	Connective	Tongue	Mouth	Ear

17. Choose the correctly matched pair.
(a) Inner lining of salivary ducts– Ciliated epithelium
(b) Moist surface of buccal cavity– Glandular epithelium
(c) Tubular parts of nephrons– Cuboidal epithelium
(d) Uriniferous tubules– Squamous epithelium

18. While doing work and running, you move your organs like hands, legs, etc. Which among the following is correct?
(a) Smooth muscles relax and push the ligament to move the bones
(b) Smooth muscles contract and pull the tendons to move the bones
(c) Skeletal muscles contract and pull the ligament to move the bones
(d) Skeletal muscles contract and pull the tendon to move the bones

19. A person met with an accident in which two long bones of his hand were dislocated. Which among the following may be the possible reasons?
(a) Tendon break
(b) Ligament break
(c) Break of skeletal muscle
(d) Areolar tissue break

20. There are two types of tissues given below with their respective codes, *A* and *B*. Consider both of these diagrams carefully and select the correct option.

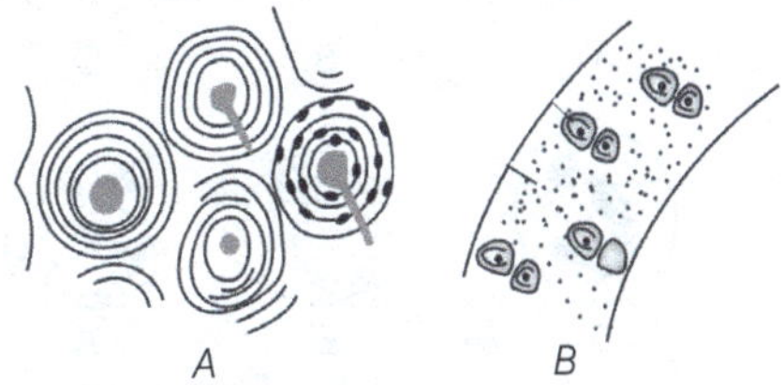

A. These are very strong and non-flexible tissue.

B. It is specialised connective tissue having fluid filled spaces called lacunae.

Codes

	A	*B*
(a)	Tendon	Cartilage
(b)	Tendon	Bone
(c)	Bone	Cartilage
(d)	Bone	Tendon

21. Complete the following flow chart.

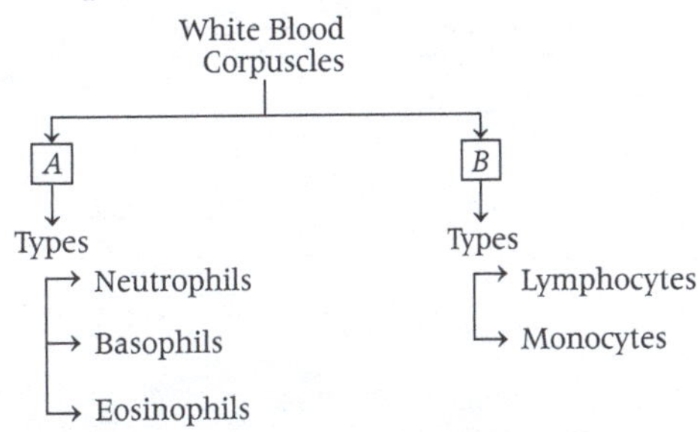

Identify *A* and *B* from the options given below

	A	*B*
(a)	Erythrocytes	Leucocytes
(b)	Granulocytes	Erythrocytes
(c)	Granulocytes	Agranulocytes
(d)	Agranulophils	Granulocytes

22. Identify the correct match of connective tissue.

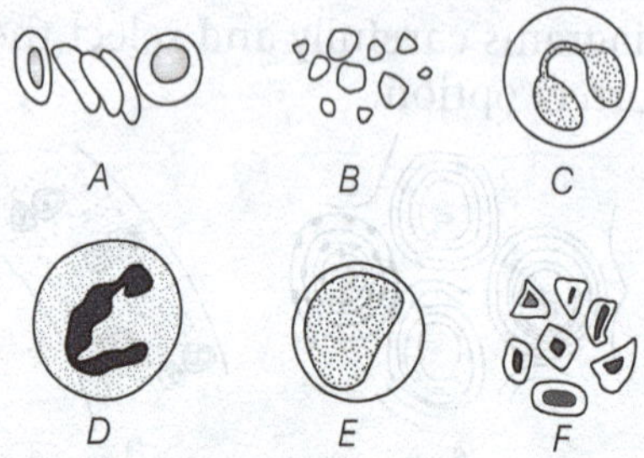

(a) *A*–RBC, *B*–Platelets, *C*–Eosinophils
(b) *F*–Platelets, *E*–Monocyte, *A*–RBC
(c) *A*–Platelets, *B*–Neutrophils, *F*–RBC
(d) *C*–Eosinophils, *D*–Basophils, *E*–RBC

23. Match the Column I with Column II.

Column I	Column II
A. RBCs	1. Antibodies
B. WBCs	2. Haemoglobin
C. Platelets	3. Blood largest part
D. Plasma	4. Clotting

Codes

	A	B	C	D		A	B	C	D
(a)	3	1	4	4	(b)	2	3	1	4
(c)	2	1	4	3	(d)	1	3	2	4

24. A person met with an accident due to which paralysis occurred in his body. He has lost motion control over some muscles of his body. But still, a few of his body organs are working.
Which muscle do you think is/are able to work even in the paralysis stage of the whole body ?
(a) Smooth muscles
(b) Cardiac muscles
(c) Both (a) and (b)
(d) None of the above

25. Arun was given a sample of tissues. He observes and concludes the following characters.
A. The cells are composed of a single layer of tall and slender cells.
B. Their nuclei are located at the base.
C. Free surface may have microvilli.
D. It is found in the lining of stomach and intestine.
E. They help in secretion and absorption.
Based on the above features identify the epithelium.
(a) Cuboidal epithelium
(b) Columnar epithelium
(c) Squamous epithelium
(d) Glandular epithelium

2 Marks Questions

26. Refer to the given Venn diagram. Identify the *A* and *C* and relation of these with *B*.

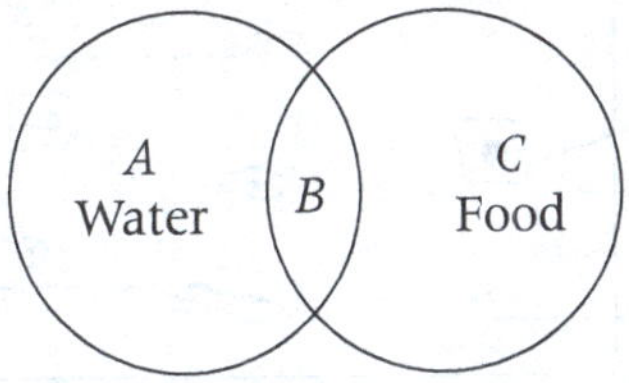

I. Tissue *A* and *C* constitute tissue *B* in plants.

II. Tissue *A* is simple tissue and tissue *C* is complex tissue.

III. Tissue *A* and *C* are complex tissue.

IV. Tissue *B* is present in animals.

Codes

(a) I and II (b) I and III

(c) Only I (d) III and IV

27. Identify the given figures and select the major difference between the structures identified.

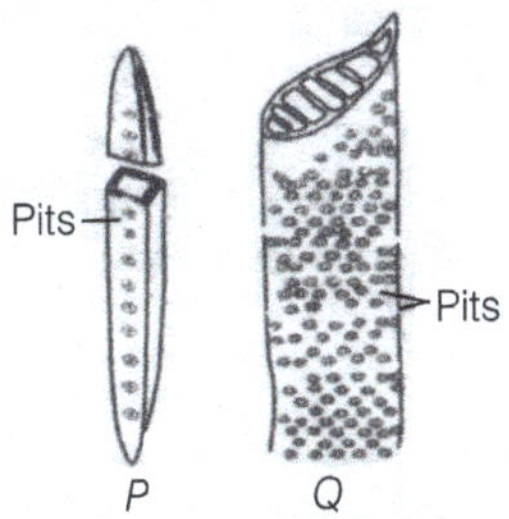

P	*Q*	Difference between *P* and *Q*
I. Vessels	Tracheids	Narrow and wide
II. Tracheids	Vessels	Unicellular, small sized and multicellular large sized.
III. Vessels	Tracheids	More lignified and less lignified
IV. Fibre	Sclereids	Short and long

Codes

(a) I and IV

(b) Only II

(c) Only III

(d) None of the above

28. Identify the correct combinations from the following table.

Type of cartilage	Nature of matrix	Location
I. Fibrous cartilage	Contain more collagen fibres	Inter-vertebral disc
II. Hyaline cartilage	Contain elastic fibres	Tip of nose
III. Elastic cartilage	Contain both collagen and elastic fibres	Epiglottis
IV. Calcified cartilage	Contain megakaryocytes	Pinna of the ear

(a) I and III

(b) II and IV

(c) III and IV

(d) I and IV

29. Refer to the given Venn diagram.

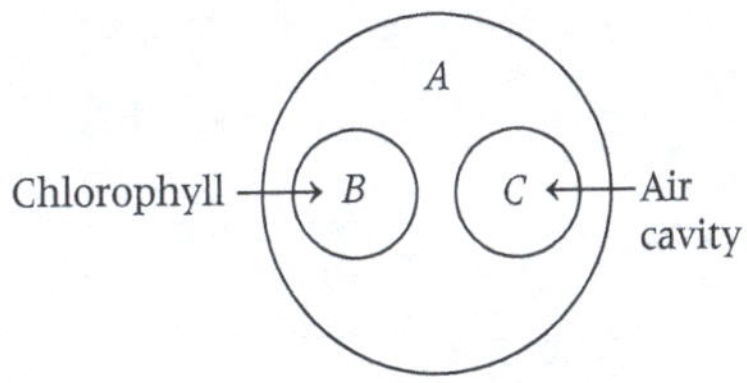

Choose the correct option.

	A	*B*	*C*
(a)	Collenchyma	Parenchyma	Sclerenchyma
(b)	Chlorenchyma	Parenchyma	Aerenchyma
(c)	Aerenchyma	Parenchyma	Chlorenchyma
(d)	Parenchyma	Chlorenchyma	Aerenchyma

30. Salman bought an indoor plant for his room. While watering the plant he noticed that water drops do not stick onto leaves of the plant and its leaves were waterproof in nature. Choose the correct options/reason for the given situation.

(a) Lignin (b) Suberin
(c) Cutin (d) Cellulose

31. Refer to the Venn diagram given below that shows different types of muscles. Identify the muscle which is labelled as A.

Which type of muscle is labelled I in the Venn diagram?

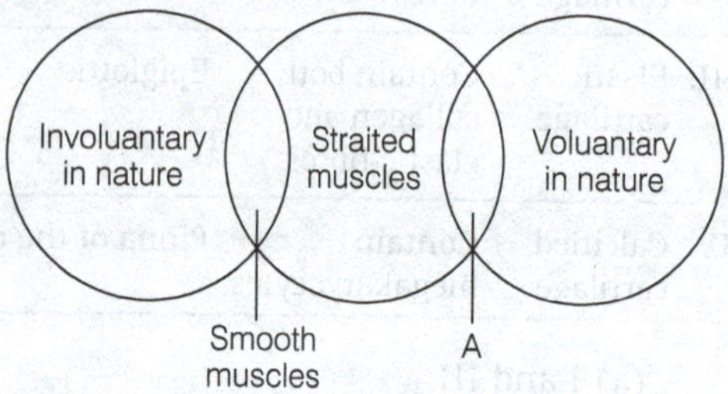

(a) Cardiac (b) Skeletal
(c) Smooth (d) None of these

32. Given below is a diagram shows a smear of human blood. Study the diagram and choose the correct label from the options given below.

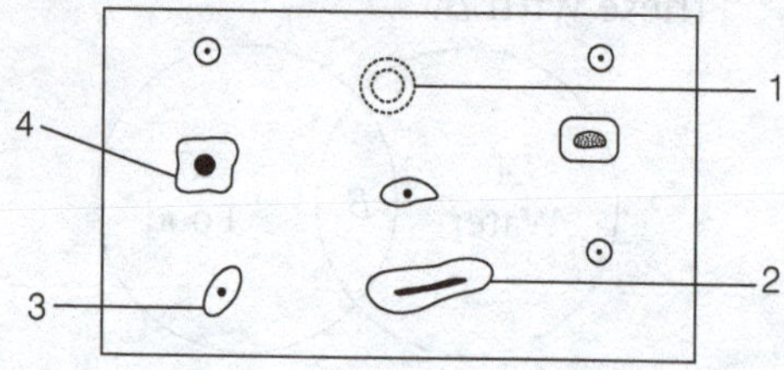

(a) 1- Red blood corpuscles 2-White blood corpuscles
3-Platelets 4-Blood plasma

(b) 1-White blood corpuscles 2-Red blood cell
3-Blood plasma 4-platelets

(c) 1-Platelets 2-Blood plasma
3- Red blood corpuscles 4-White blood corpuscles

(d) 1-Red blood corpuscles 2-Blood plasma
3-Whte blood corpuscles 4-Platelets

Chapter 07

Motion

1 Mark Questions

1. A car driver takes a total of 2 h to make a journey of 75 km. She has a coffee break of half an hour and spends a quarter of an hour stationary in a traffic jam.

   At what average speed must she travel during the rest of the time if she wants to complete the journey in the 2 h?

   (a) 38 km/h (b) 50 km/h
   (c) 60 km/h (d) 75 km/h

2. Two identical balls are at rest side by side at the bottom of a hill. The ball *A* is kicked up the hill after sometime, the ball *B* is given a kick up the hill also. Ball *A* is headed downhill when it passes ball *B* headed up the hill. At the instant when ball *A* passes ball *B*, it has the same

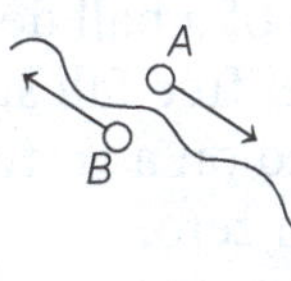

   (a) position and velocity as ball *B*
   (b) position and acceleration as ball *B*
   (c) velocity and acceleration as ball *B*
   (d) displacement and acceleration as ball *B*

3. An experiment is carried out by an astronaut on the surface of the moon. A coin and a feather are dropped at the same instant from the same height. Which statement is correct about the experiment?

   (a) The coin falls faster than the feather, but both take a longer time than if they were falling from the same height on the Earth
   (b) The coin falls faster than the feather but both take a shorter time than if they were falling from the same height on the Earth
   (c) They fall together, but the feather will take a longer time than the coin in falling from the same height on the Earth
   (d) They fall together but the feather will take a shorter time than the coin would in falling from the same height on the Earth.

4. The speed of a body during 20 s of motion is represented by the speed-time graph shown.

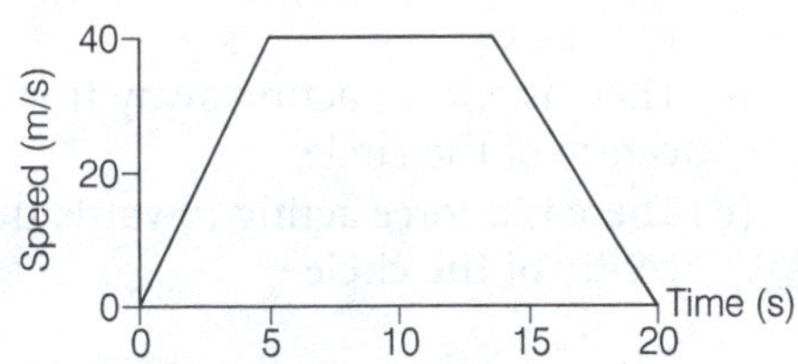

What distance does the body travel during this motion?

(a) 300 m
(b) 400 m
(c) 500 m
(d) 600 m

5. A racing car is fitted with an electronic monitoring system. Data from the car are used to plot a speed-time graph for part of the race.

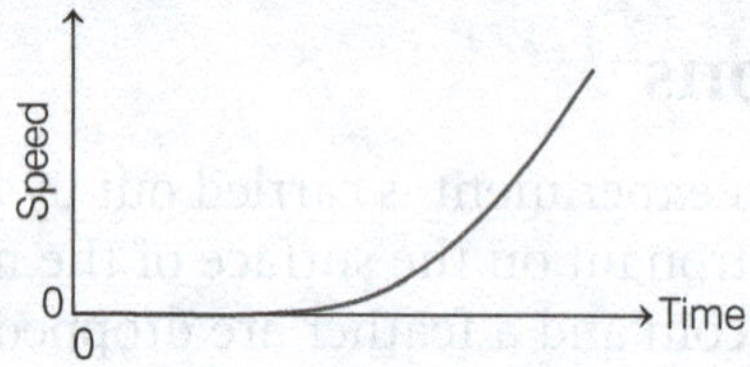

The graph is displayed on a computer screen. The graph covers a period of time when the car is first at rest, then

(a) moving with a uniform speed and then moving with uniform acceleration
(b) moving with a uniform speed and then moving with non-uniform acceleration
(c) moving with a uniform acceleration and then moving with non-uniform acceleration
(d) moving with non-uniform acceleration and then moving with a uniform acceleration

6. A body is moving in a circle at a constant speed. Which of the following statements about the body is true?

(a) There is no acceleration
(b) There is a force acting at a tangent to the circle
(c) There is a force acting away from the centre of the circle
(d) There is a force acting towards the centre of the circle

7. The angular velocity of the minute's hand of a clock is

Clock

(a) $\pi/180$ rad/s (b) $\pi/1800$ rad/s
(c) $\pi/60$ rad/s (d) $\pi/360$ rad/s

8. A particle is acted upon by a constant force, the direction of which is always perpendicular to the velocity of the particle. The motion of the particle takes place in a plane.

It follows that

(a) its velocity is constant
(b) its magnitude of acceleration is constant
(c) its KE is constant and it is in circular motion
(d) Both (b) and (c)

9. For an electron revolving around the atomic nucleus, the necessary centripetal force is provided by

(a) electrostatic force of attraction
(b) electrostatic force of repulsion
(c) nuclear charge
(d) All of the above

10. A photographer arranges to expose photographs of a ball describing motion under free fall such that it is photographed on a vertical scale starting from zero.

He photographed it when the ball was at 75 m and the next exposure was when the ball was at 80 m. The time of exposure is [$g = 10\ m/s^2$]

(a) 0.2 s (b) 0.5 s (c) 1 s (d) 1.5 s

11. Points P, Q and R are in a vertical line such that $PQ = QR$. A ball at the topmost point P is allowed to fall freely. What is the ratio of the times of descent through PQ and QR?

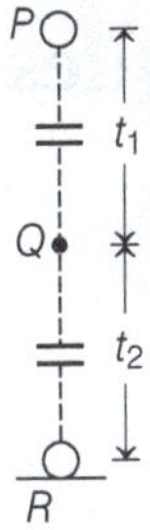

(a) $\frac{3}{2}$ (b) $\frac{3}{\sqrt{2}+1}$

(c) $\frac{1}{\sqrt{2}-1}$ (d) $\frac{5}{2}$

12. Two bodies of different masses m_a and m_b are dropped from two different heights a and b, respectively. The ratio of the time taken by the two to drop through these distances is

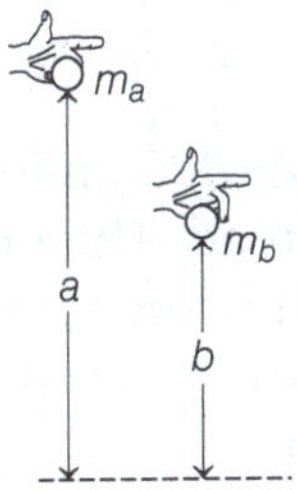

(a) $a:b$ (b) $b:a$

(c) $\sqrt{a}:\sqrt{b}$ (d) $a^2:b^2$

13. Two stones are thrown from the top of a building with the same speed u one in upward direction and the other in downward direction. When they reach ground, they acquire certain velocities v_1 and v_2, respectively. v_1 and v_2 will be in the ratio of

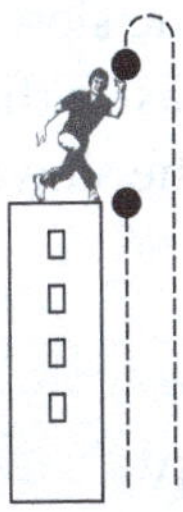

(a) 1 : 1 (b) 1 : 2

(c) 2 : 1 (d) 2 : 3

14. A body is left free on a frictionless inclined plane as shown in the figure. It takes 2 s to reach the bottom of the plank. What time would it take to slide from point A to point B?

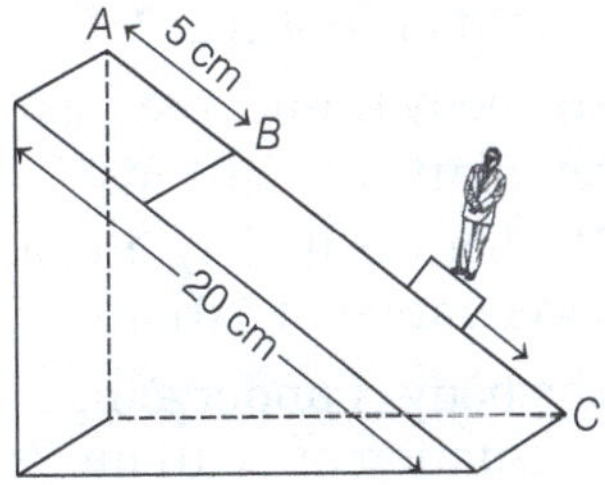

(a) 0.5 s (b) 1 s (c) 1.5 s (d) 2 s

15. A particle with a uniform acceleration in a straight line has a speed of v ms^{-1} at position x metres is given by $v = \sqrt{50 - 8x}$. The acceleration of the particle is

(a) 50 ms^{-2} (b) 25 ms^{-2}

(c) -8 ms^{-2} (d) -4 ms^{-2}

16. Two scooters starting from rest accelerate uniformly at the same rate. The second scooter travels twice the time of the first scooter. Then, the relation between the distance covered by the first scooter (s_1) to that of second scooter (s_2) is

(a) $s_1 = s_2$ (b) $s_1 = 2s_2$

(c) $s_2 = 3s_1$ (d) $s_2 = 4s_1$

17. Which of the following statements is/are correct?

I. The motion of the Earth around the Sun once every year requires same force of attraction between them.

II. The centripetal force acting between Sun and Earth is the gravitational force between them.

Codes

(a) Only I (b) Only II

(c) Both I and II (d) None of these

2 Marks Questions

18. The velocity of a body is given by the equation $v = 8 - 0.01t$, where t is the time taken. Then, which of the given statements is not true?

I. The body is undergoing a uniform retardation of 0.01 ms^{-2}.

II. The body is undergoing a uniform acceleration of 0.01 ms^{-2}.

III. The body is undergoing a uniform retardation of –0.01 ms^{-2}.

IV. The body is undergoing a uniform a acceleration of 0.08 ms^{-2}.

Codes

(a) I and II (b) III and IV

(c) I, II and III (d) II, III and IV

19. The distances travelled by a body falling freely from rest in the first, second and third seconds respectively are in the ratio of

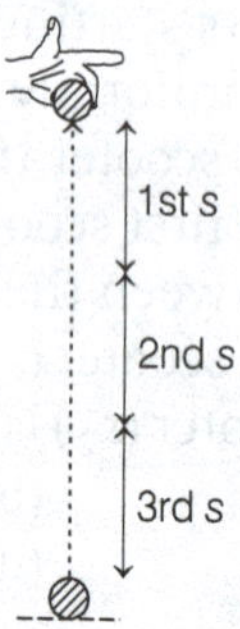

(a) 1 : 4 : 9 (b) 1 : 2 : 3

(c) 1 : 9 : 25 (d) 1 : 3 : 5

20. State [T] for True or [F] for False.

I. The direction of acceleration due to gravity is always vertically downwards.

II. The ratio of heights from which two bodies are dropped is 3 : 5 respectively. The ratio of their final velocities is $\sqrt{5} : \sqrt{3}$.

III. A freely falling body means a body whose acceleration is equal to acceleration due to gravity but its initial velocity may or may not be zero.

IV. Heavier body falls with greater acceleration.

V. Time of flight depends upon the mass of the bodies.

Codes

	I	II	III	IV	V
(a)	T	T	F	F	F
(b)	F	F	T	T	F
(c)	T	F	T	F	F
(d)	F	T	F	T	T

21. Four cars *A*, *B*, *C* and *D* are moving on a levelled road. Their distance *versus* time graph is shown in figure. Which of the given statements are not correct?

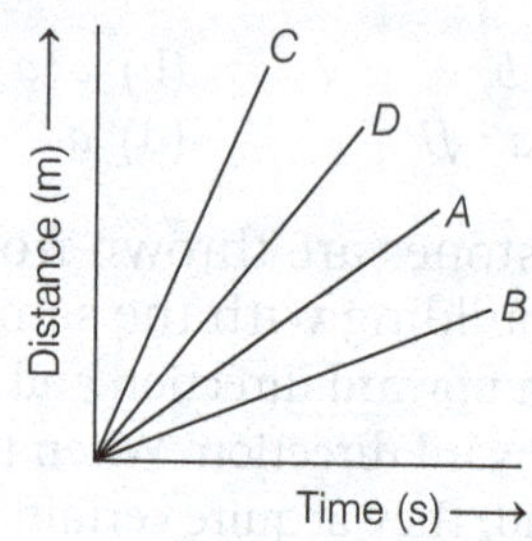

I. Car *A* is faster than car *D*.

II. Car *B* is the slowest.

III. Car *D* is faster than car *C*.

IV. Car *C* is the slowest.

Codes

(a) I and II

(b) III and IV

(c) I, III and IV

(d) II, III and IV

Chapter 08

Force and Laws of Motion

1 Mark Questions

1. Rahim is opening the tap to fill his bucket with water. While opening the tap, what must be the essential condition?

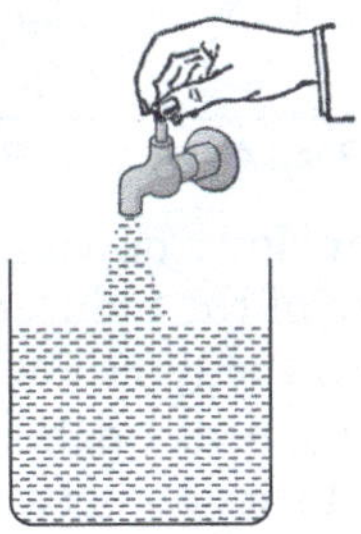

I. The forces equal in magnitude.
II. The forces parallel to each other.
III. The forces opposite in direction.

Codes

(a) I and II (b) Only III
(c) II and III (d) I, II and III

2. Jason applied a force to an inflated balloon placed on a table. Which of the following is/are possible observation(s) after he had applied the force?

I. The balloon burst.
II. The mass of balloon increased.
III. The balloon dropped onto the floor from the table.
IV. The balloon remained at the same position on the table.

Codes

(a) Only I (b) Only II
(c) I and III (d) I and IV

3. Which of the statement(s) is/are correct?

I. Smaller objects are always lighter.
II. Gravity affects the weight of an object.
III. The effect of weight cannot be felt but can be seen.
IV. The weight of an object depends on its mass only.

Codes

(a) Only II (b) I and II
(c) III and IV (d) II, III and IV

4. Simi conducted an experiment with 3 balls of same size. She attached the balls with a piece of string each and hung them at the same height. She then cut the strings and let the balls drop onto a bar of plasticine as shown below.

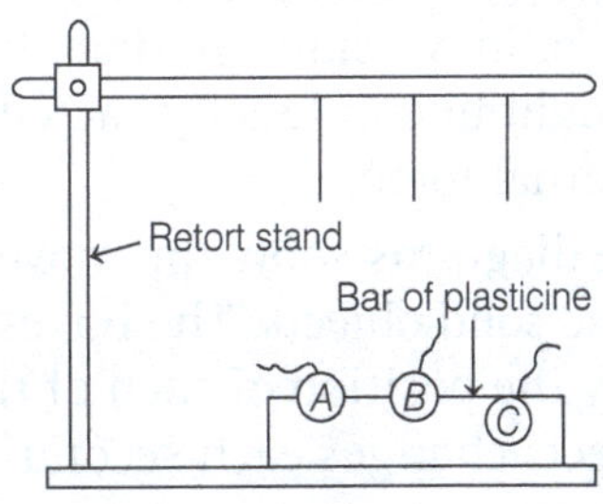

Which one of the following deductions is correct?

(a) Ball *C* has the greatest mass
(b) Ball *A* has the greatest mass
(c) Ball *B* has the greatest mass
(d) Balls *A*, *B* and *C* have the same mass

5. Uncle Joe was picking up some boxes as shown below.

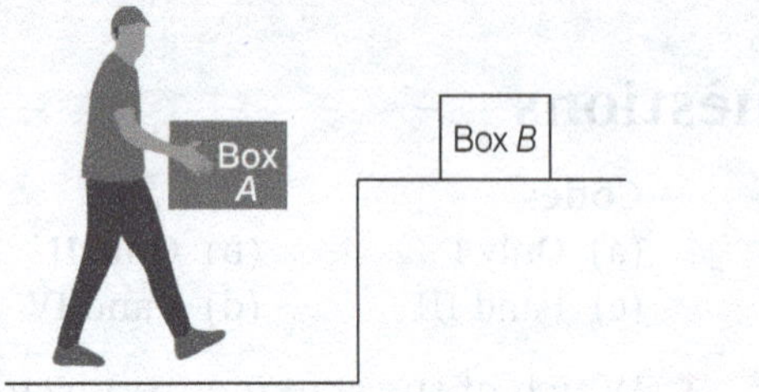

Which of the following statement(s) about the forces involved is/are correct?

I. Box *B* was stationary so there was no force acting on it.
II. Box *A* was lifted easily due to higher upward force than gravity acting on it.
III. The gravitational force on box *A* was more than box *B*, since it was at a lower position.
IV. There were equal amount of forces acting on both boxes in the diagram above.

Codes

(a) Only II (b) I and II
(c) I, II and III (d) I, II, III and IV

6. An object remains either in a state of rest or in constant motion along a straight line unless it is acted on by a external force.

The diagrams show the movement of some solid objects. The boxes show how the position of each of the objects changes each second.

Which of these diagrams shows an object subjected to a balanced external force?

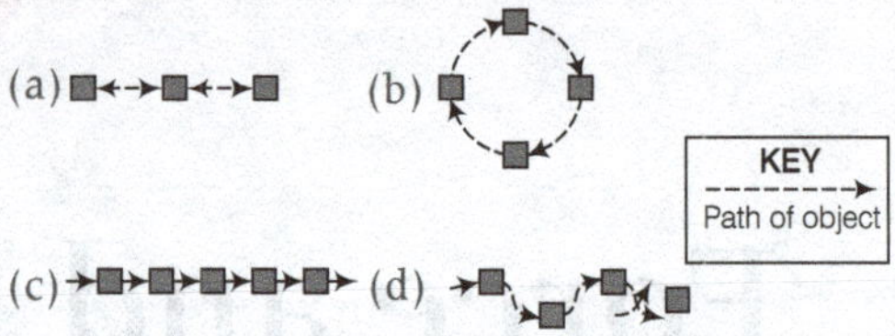

7. John while going to home from office has to pass through road *A* and road *B*. He stops at both the roads to collect fruits for home.

Compared to breaking on road *A* what may happen on road *B*?

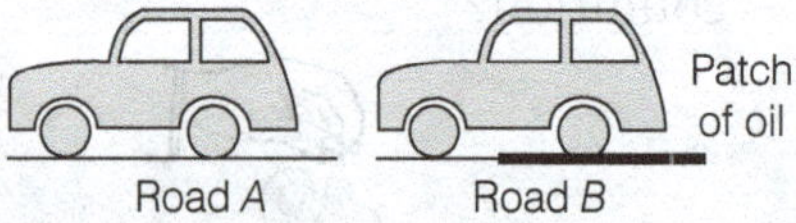

(a) The car slows down more quickly, because of the reduced friction between the tyres and the road
(b) The car speeds up, because of the reduced friction between the tyres and the road
(c) The car takes longer to slow down, because of the reduced friction between the tyres and the road
(d) The car takes longer to slow down, because of the greater friction between the tyres and the road

8. Vehicles are provided with shock absorbers, a mechanical device designed to smooth out or damp shock impulses and convert kinetic energy to another form of energy usually thermal energy which can be dissipated. Shock absorbers obey Newton's

(a) first law of motion
(b) second law of motion
(c) third law of motion
(d) All of the above

9. 

Water tanker

A water tanker filled up to 2/3 of its height is moving with a uniform speed. On sudden application of the brakes, the water level in the tank will be as

(a) 
(b) 
(c) 
(d) 

10. Trolley X and trolley Y are joined with stretched spring. Trolley X has twice the mass of trolley Y.

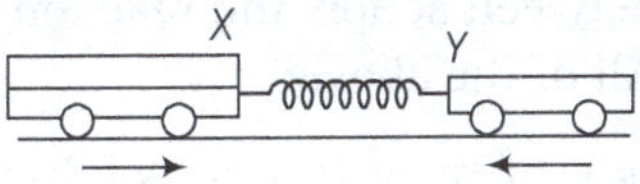

When the trolleys are released, the acceleration of X is $2\ m/s^2$ to the right. What is the initial acceleration of trolley Y to the left?

(a) $1\ m/s^2$ (b) $2\ m/s^2$
(c) $3\ m/s^2$ (d) $4\ m/s^2$

11. A person just supports a mass of 20 kg suspended from a rope.

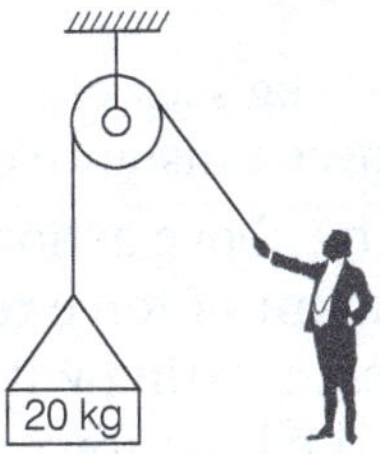

What is the resultant force acting on the mass?

(a) Zero (b) 10 N
(c) 20 N (d) 200 N

12. A block of mass 6 kg is pulled across a rough surface by a 54 N force against a friction force F.

The acceleration of the block is $6\ m/s^2$. What is the value of F?

(a) 9 N (b) 18 N
(c) 36 N (d) 54 N

13. During a planned manoeuvre in a space flight, a free floating astronaut A pushes another free floating astronaut B, the mass of A being greater than that of B. Then, the magnitude of the force exerted by astronaut A on astronaut B is

(a) equal to zero
(b) equal to the force exerted by B on A
(c) greater than the force exerted by B on A
(d) less than the force exerted by B on A

14. Figure shows the displacement of a particle going along the X-axis as function of time. The force acting on the particle is zero in the region.

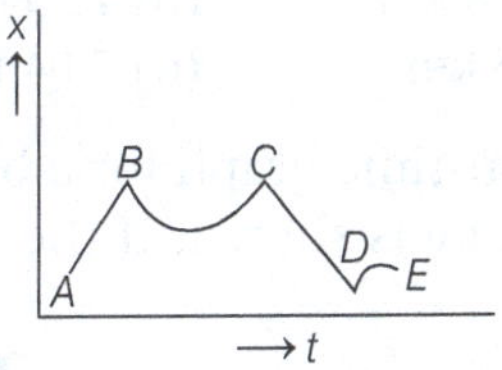

(a) AB (b) BC
(c) CE (d) DE

15. Study the figure given below and assuming the force to be constant, its magnitude is

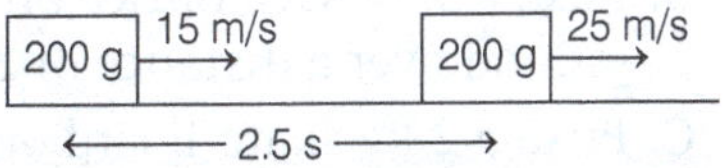

(a) 0.4 N (b) 0.6 N
(c) 0.8 N (d) 0.5 N

16. Which of the following statement is/are correct?

I. Newton's third law of motion is applicable only when bodies are in motion.

II. Newton's third law applies to all types of forces, e.g. gravitational, electric or magnetic, etc.

Codes

(a) Only I (b) Only II
(c) Both I and II (c) None of these

17. An object of mass 4 kg starting from origin at $t = 0$ with a speed of 20 m/s in the positive direction of x-axis. If a force of 10 N acts on the object towards the negative x-axis. The position of the object after 2s will be

(a) 40 m (b) 50 m (c) 35 m (d) 65 m

18. An object of mass 200 g is moving along the positive direction of x-axis with speed of 4 m/s. If its speed is increased to double under the effect of a constant applying force of 10 N, then position of the object after 20 s will be

(a) 10.08 km (b) 12.54 km
(c) 6.56 km (d) 5.04 km

19. Position-time graph for a body of mass 2 kg is shown. If the forces on the body for $t < 0, 0 < t < 6\text{s}$ and $t > 6\text{s}$ are F_1, F_2 and F_3 respectively, then

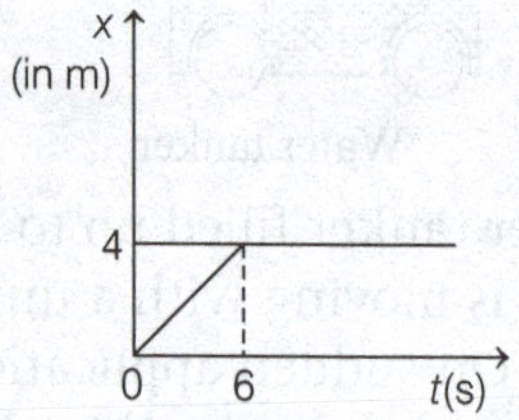

(a) $F_1 = F_2 > F_3$
(b) $F_1 = F_3 > F_2$
(c) $F_1 > F_2 > F_3$
(d) $F_1 = F_2 = F_3$

20. Choose the correct one with respect to Newton's third law of motion.

(a) Action and reaction always act on the different bodies
(b) Action and reaction forces are simultaneous forces
(c) There is no cause effect relationship between action and reaction
(d) All of the above

21. A book of weight 3 kg is lying on the table. If $g = 10\ \text{m/s}^2$, then reaction force on the table and the angle between the action of the book on the table and reaction of the table on the book are, respectively.

(a) 30 N, 0° (b) 3N, 180°
(c) 30 N, 180° (d) 3 N, 0°

2 Marks Questions

22. Study the following actions that were carried out.

A. Push a 2 kg bag of flour on a flat ground over a distance of 2 m.
B. Push a 5 kg sack of rice on a flat ground over a distance of 2 m.
C. Push a 2 kg skate-board on a flat ground over a distance of 2 m.
D. Push a 5 kg sack of onions up a slope over a distance of 2 m.

Arrange the above actions according to the amount of force required for each action, starting with the action that uses the least force.

(a) C, A, D, B (b) C, A, B, D
(c) D, B, A, C (d) D, C, A, B

23. A can filled with sand is hung on a long string close to the surface of the Earth. An identical can is hung in the same way close to the surface of the Moon. The cans are given a sideways push.

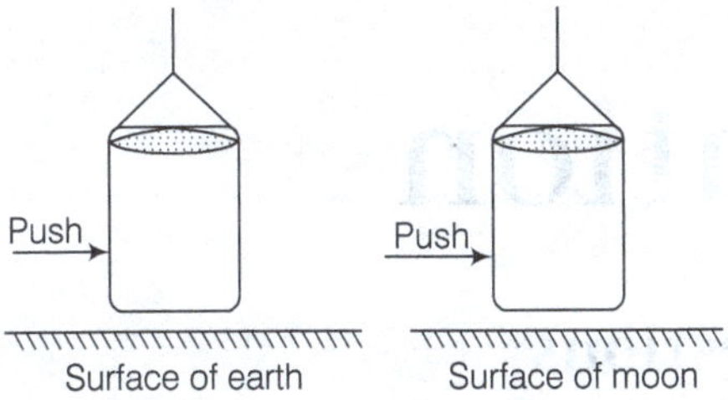

Compared with the can hanging close to the Earth, the can close to the moon starts to move

(a) more easily, as it has less mass
(b) more easily, as it has less weight
(c) with the same ease, as it has the same mass
(d) with the same ease, as it has the same weight

24. A ball of mass 2 kg drops vertically on a floor hitting with a speed of 20 m/s. It rebounds with an initial speed of 10 m/s. If the ball was in contact for only 0.04 s, then force exerted on the floor by the ball is

(a) 1000 N (b) 1500 N
(c) 2000 N (d) 500 N

25. An aircraft flying at a constant height is gaining speed. The four forces acting are

L : lift due to the wings

R : air resistance

T : the thrust due to the engines

W : the weight

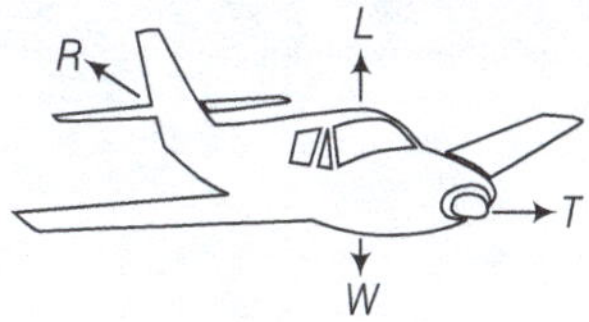

What is correct relation?

	Vertical forces	Horizontal forces
(a)	$L = W$	$T = R$
(b)	$L > W$	$T > R$
(c)	$L = W$	$T > R$
(d)	$L > W$	$T = R$

26. State [T] for True or [F] for False.

I. Impulse and momentum have same unit.
II. If two bodies of different masses move with the same momentum, then heavier body will have greater velocity.
III. Walking is more easier on the ground than on sand. In the former case, the reaction comes into play more quickly.
IV. The area under F-t graph gives a acceleration.
V. A force must act on a vehicle moving on a rough road in a straight line with a uniform velocity.

Codes

	I	II	III	IV	V		I	II	III	IV	V
(a)	F	T	F	T	F	(b)	T	T	F	F	F
(c)	T	F	T	F	T	(d)	F	F	T	F	T

Chapter 09

Gravitation

1 Mark Questions

1. A team of astronauts went to Moon to study physical conditions on Moon. In one of their experiment, they made two objects of different masses fall freely near the surface of the Moon. What results they may have obtained?

(a) The two objects have same velocity at any instant

(b) The two objects have different accelerations

(c) The two objects experience forces of same magnitude

(d) The two objects undergo a change in their inertia

2. Which of the following is true in relation to the value of acceleration due to gravity?

I. It is same on equator and poles.

II. It is least on poles.

III. It is least on equator.

IV. It increases from pole to equator.

Codes

(a) I and II (b) Only III

(c) III and IV (d) I, II and IV

3. The weight of a body is the force with which a body is attracted by the earth towards its centre. What is the weight of an object at the point *A* shown in figure?

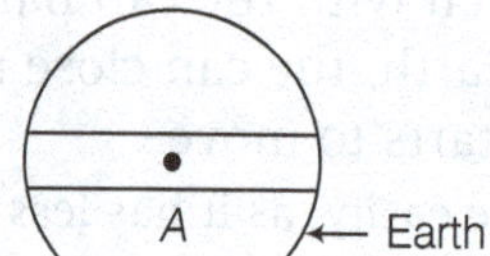

(a) Zero

(b) Infinite

(c) *R* times the weight at the surface of the earth

(d) $1/R^2$ times the weight at the surface of the earth

4. Consider the following diagrams.

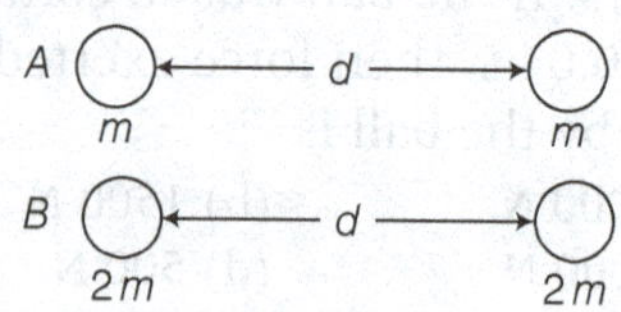

If the gravitational force for system *A* is *F*, then what will be the gravitational force for system *B*?

(a) $\frac{1}{4}F$ (b) $4F$

(c) $\frac{1}{2}F$ (d) Unchanged

5. Aditya weighed his laptop on a weighing machine at the north pole. The reading on the machine was 49. What was the mass of his laptop? How will the weight of the laptop be changed if weighed at the equator?

(a) 7 kg, weight of laptop increases
(b) 5 kg, weight of laptop increases
(c) 5 kg, weight of laptop decreases
(d) 5 kg, weight of laptop remains unchanged

6. Consider the following picture.

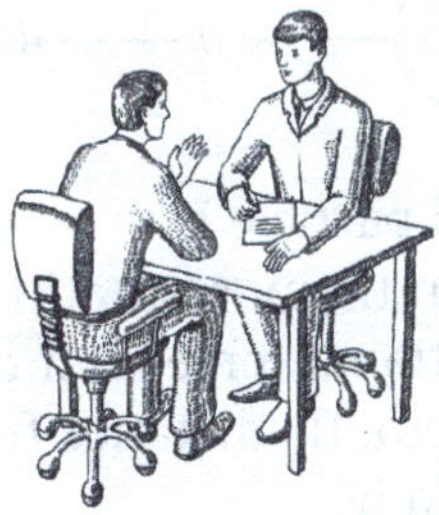

The value of gravitational force between two friends of masses 60 kg each is closest to

(a) 10^{-7} N (b) 1 N (c) 10^{4} N (d) 10^{7} N

7. Given below are two protons.

What will be the gravitational force between them?

(Take, 1 femtometre $=10^{-15}$ m, mass of a proton $=1.67\times 10^{-27}$ kg.)

(a) 1.86×10^{-34} N (b) 5.86×10^{-34} N
(c) 2.8×10^{-34} N (d) 4.86×10^{-34} N

8. Communication satellites move in the orbits of radius 44400 km around the Earth. Assuming that only the gravitational force acting on it. The acceleration of the satellite is ($M_e=6\times 10^{24}$ kg)

(a) 0.4 ms^{-2} (b) 0.6 ms^{-2}
(c) 0.2 ms^{-2} (d) 0.1 ms^{-2}

9. Consider a heavenly body which has a mass twice that of the Earth and a radius thrice that of the Earth. The weight of a book on this heavenly body if its weight on the Earth is 900 N will be

(a) 400 N (b) 600 N (c) 500 N (d) 200 N

10. Consider a heavenly body whose mass is 3×10^{24} kg (half of that of the earth) and radius is 3200 km (half of that of the Earth). The acceleration due to gravity at the surface of this heavenly body will be

(a) 39.6 m/s^2 (b) 19.6 m/s^2
(c) 29.6 m/s^2 (d) 49.6 m/s^2

11. The mass of a planet is twice and its radius is 3 times that of the Earth. The weight of a body which has a mass of 5 kg on the surface of that planet is

(a) 11.95 N (b) 20.9 N
(c) 10.85 N (d) 9.9 N

12. If the diameter of Earth becomes two times of its present value and its mass remains unchanged, then how would the weight of an object on the surface of the Earth be affected?

(a) Weight would become one-third
(b) Weight would become one-fourth
(c) Weight would become one-fifth
(d) Weight would become one-sixth

13. An astronaut on the Moon measures the acceleration due to gravity to be 1.7 ms^{-2}. He knows that the radius of the Moon is about 0.27 times that of the Earth. What is his estimate of the ratio of the mass of the Earth to that of the Moon? (The acceleration due to gravity on the Earth's surface is 9.8 ms^{-2}).

(a) 67 (b) 58 (c) 46 (d) 79

14. If the radius of the Earth shrinks by 4% and there is no change in its mass, then acceleration due to gravity, which depends on mass and radius will change. By how much does the value of g change?

(a) 2% (b) 4% (c) 16% (d) 8%

2 Marks Questions

15. Which of the following is not true for universal gravitational constant?

I. It depends on the value of g at the place of observation.

II. It is used only when the Earth is one of the two masses.

III. It is greatest at the surface of the Earth.

IV. It is universal constant of nature.

Codes

(a) I and II (b) III and IV

(c) I, II and III (d) I, III and IV

16. An apple falls from a tree because of gravitational force of attraction F_1 between the Earth and apple. If F_2 is the magnitude of force exerted by apple on the Earth, then

(a) $F_1 >> F_2$ (b) $F_2 >> F_1$

(c) $F_1 > F_2$ (d) $F_1 = F_2$

17. If we go inside a mine and drop a 10 kg iron ball and 1 kg aluminium ball from the top of a high platform, then which of the following is not true?

I. Both will reach the floor at the same time.

II. 1 kg weight will reach the floor first.

III. 10 kg weight will reach the floor first.

IV. It is not possible to indicate which of the two will reach the floor first without further data.

Codes

(a) Only I

(b) II and IV

(c) I, II and III

(d) II, III and IV

18. Two bodies A and B are placed at distance d from each other as shown in figure below.

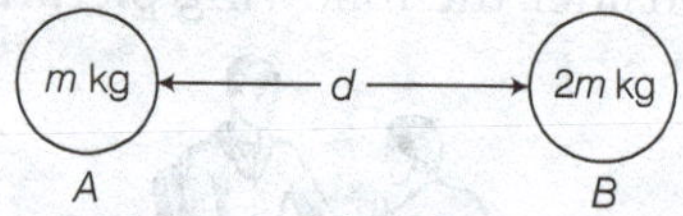

A small particle is to be placed between them, so that the net gravitational force on it due to A and B are zero. Its distance from the mass A should be

(a) $x = \frac{d}{1+\sqrt{2}}$ (b) $x = \frac{d}{1+\sqrt{4}}$

(c) $x = \frac{d}{1+\sqrt{3}}$ (d) $x = \frac{d}{1+\sqrt{6}}$

19. A team of astronaut experiments in a body, which was suspended from a spring balance kept in a satellite. The reading of the spring balance was w_1 when the satellite goes in an orbit of radius R and w_2 when it goes in an orbit of radius 2 R. Which of the following option is correct for the above experiment?

(a) $w_1 = w_2$ (b) $w_1 < w_2$

(c) $w_1 > w_2$ (d) $w_1 \neq w_2$

20. 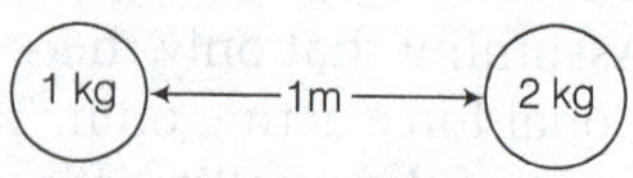

What will be the acceleration of the bodies in the above system, assuming that only gravitational force acts between them?

(a) 1.33×10^{-10} m/s^2 and 6.67×10^{-11} m/s^2

(b) 1.33×10^{-11} m/s^2 and 6.25×10^{-11} m/s^2

(c) 5.36×10^{-11} m/s^2 and 5.26×10^{-11} m/s^2

(d) 3.11×10^{-11} m/s^2 and 5.26×10^{-11} m/s^2

Chapter 10

Work and Energy

1 Mark Questions

1. Which of the following statement(s) is/are true about the positive work done by an object?

I. The object must stop.

II. The object must move in the direction of the force applied.

III. There must be a force acting on an object.

IV. The object must move in the direction opposite to the direction of the force applied.

Codes

(a) I and II
(b) II and III
(c) I, II and III
(d) I, II and IV

2. Work is done when an object moves

I. at an angle 90° to the direction of force.

II. at an angle opposite to the direction of force.

III. at any angle to the direction of force.

IV. along the direction of force.

Codes

(a) II, III and IV
(b) I, II and IV
(c) I, III and IV
(d) III and IV

3. Two boxes *P* and *Q* of the same weight were lifted from the ground to two different heights using a rope.

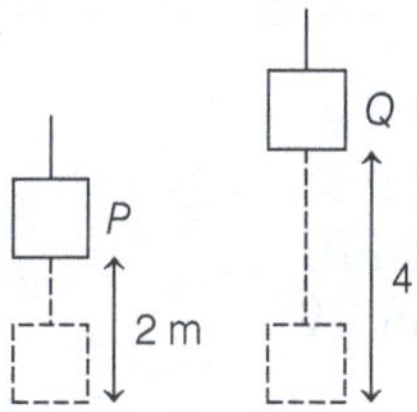

Which of the following is not true about the work done by the boxes?

I. Box *P* did more work than box *Q*.

II. Box *P* did not do any work.

III. Box *Q* did more work than box *P*.

IV. Since, both boxes were lifted vertically up, they did not do any work.

Codes

(a) I and II (b) II and III
(c) I, II and III (d) I, II and IV

4. The diagram below shows ball *P* moving and colliding with ball *Q* which is stationary.

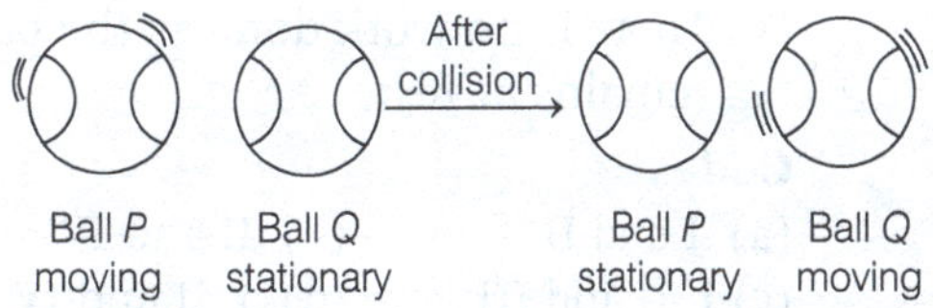

After ball P collides with ball Q, ball P remained stationary and ball Q started to roll.

Which of the following statements is/are not correct about the collision?

I. There is no work done by ball P because it stops moving after collision.

II. Work is done only by ball Q as it moves towards the direction of the force.

III. Work is done by both the balls as there was a transfer of energy between them.

IV. There was no work done by both the balls.

Codes

(a) Only I

(b) II and IV

(c) I, II and III

(d) I, II and IV

5. The diagram shows two forces acting on a ball in opposite directions.

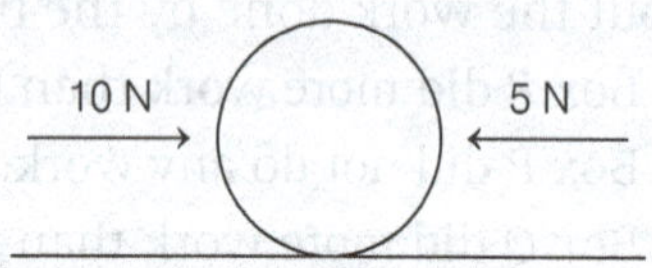

Which of the following statements is/are not correct?

I. There is no work done because there are two forces acting in opposite direction.

II. Work is said to be done as the ball will move to the left.

III. Work is said to be done as the ball will move to the right.

IV. There is no work done as the ball remains at rest.

Codes

(a) I and II (b) II and IV

(c) I, II and III (d) I, II and IV

6. A centripetal force is a force that makes a body follow a curved path. Its direction is always orthogonal to the velocity of the body and towards the fixed point of the instantaneous centre of curvature of path.

Which of the following statements is not correct regarding the relation between centripetal force and radius of the circular path?

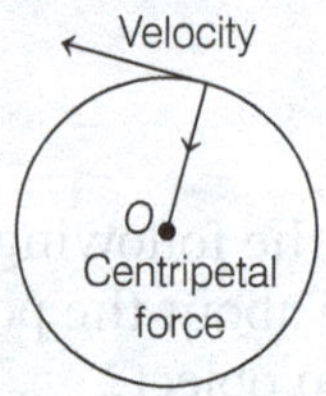

I. Work done by the centripetal force increases, if the radius of the path is increased.

II. Work done by the centripetal force decreases by decreasing the radius.

III. Work done by the centripetal force increases by decreasing the radius.

IV. Work done is always zero.

Codes

(a) I and II (b) I, II and III

(c) II and IV (d) II, III and IV

7. The diagram shows a small car of mass 500 kg approaching a hill. It moves up the hill with a uniform speed.

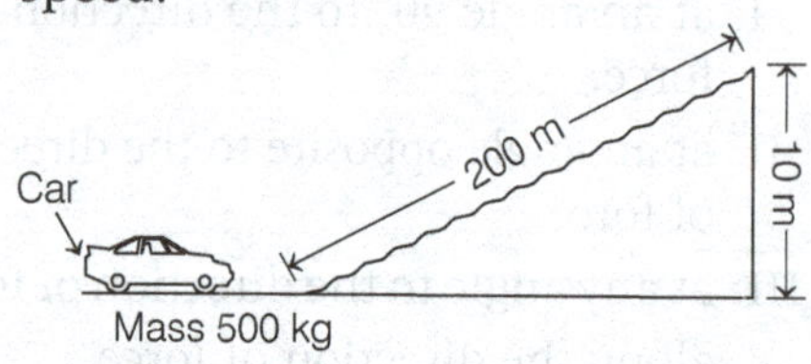

Ignore friction and take the value of g to be 10 N/kg. How much work is done in moving the car up the hill

(a) 5×10^3 J (b) 5×10^4 J

(c) 1×10^5 J (d) 1×10^6 J

8. Sarthak while practising for shooting fires a bullet from his gun with velocity v. Mass of the bullet is m. The mass of the gun is M and it recoils with velocity v. If the kinetic energy of the bullet is E_b and that of gun be E_g, then

(a) $E_b = E_g$
(b) $E_b < E_g$
(c) $E_b > E_g$
(d) $E_b \geq E_g$

9. A ball is thrown upwards from a point A. It reaches up to a highest point B and returns. Here,

I. kinetic energy at A = kinetic energy at B
II. potential energy at A = potential energy at B
III. potential energy at B = kinetic energy at B
IV. potential energy at B = kinetic energy at A

Codes

(a) Only II (b) Only IV
(c) I and II (d) III and IV

10. Nicole's bicycle has a dynamo (a small electrical generator) and a lamp. As she pedals, the dynamo spins and her lamp lights up, helping her to see at night.

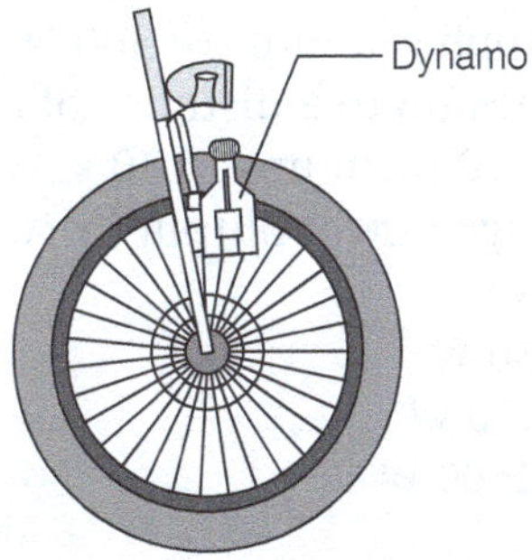

Front wheel of Nicole's bicycle

Which of the following correctly shows the energy conversions that occur?

(a) Electrical energy → kinetic energy + light energy + heat energy
(b) Kinetic energy → chemical potential energy → light energy
(c) Kinetic energy → electrical energy → light energy + heat energy
(d) Chemical potential energy → electrical energy + light energy

11. Look at the set up below. Which of the boxes will make a deeper depression in the sand if the rope is cut?

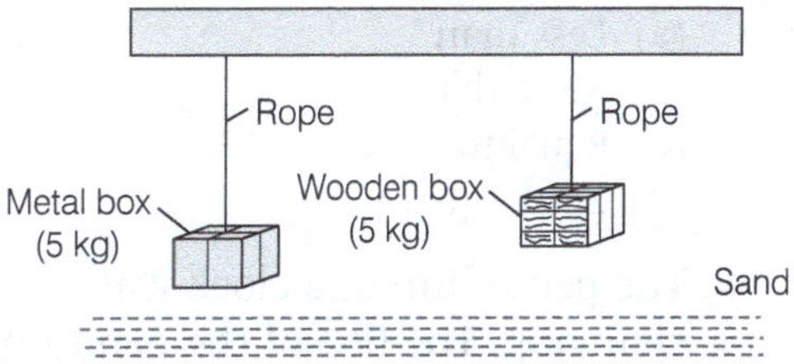

(a) The metal box
(b) The wooden box
(c) They will make identical depressions
(d) Neither of them will make a depression in the sand

12. A lorry and a car moving on a horizontal road in opposite direction with the same kinetic energy were about to collide. The drivers of both lorry and car applied brakes which provide equal retarding forces. Which of them will come to rest in a shorter distance?

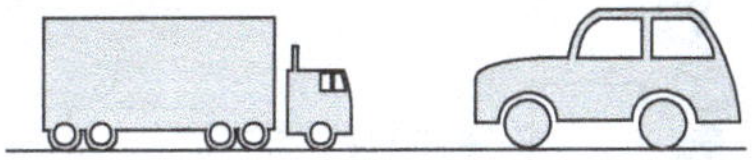

(a) Lorry
(b) Car
(c) Both will stop at the same distance
(d) None of the above

13. A man carrying a bag of sand, is walking at a constant speed. There is a hole in the bag and sand is continuously falling out.

His kinetic energy at point *B* will be how much of his kinetic energy at point *A*?

(a) Less than
(b) More than
(c) Equal to
(d) Zero, equal to

14. The pendulum of a clock was swinging. The bob of the pendulum passes through its mean and extreme position repeatedly. Calculate the velocity of the bob of a simple pendulum at mean position if it is able to rise to a vertical height of 10 cm. (Given, $g = 980 \text{ cm s}^{-2}$)

(a) 1.40 ms^{-1} (b) 2.54 ms^{-1}
(c) 3.43 ms^{-1} (d) 5.35 ms^{-1}

15. Anuj pushes a box and applied a force of 300 N on the box weighing 600 N, the box moves 3.0 m horizontally in 20 s.

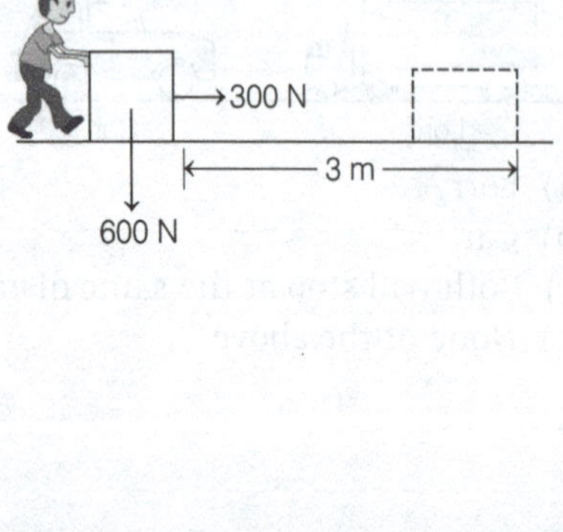

What is the average power?

(a) 45 W (b) 90 W
(c) 900 W (d) 1800 W

16. A girl of weight 500N runs up a flight of stairs in 10s. The vertical height of the stairs is 5m.

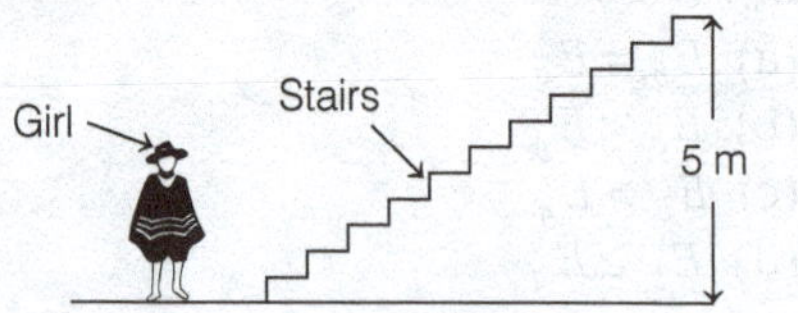

What is the average power developed by the girl?

(a) 50 W (b) 100 W
(c) 250 W (d) 1000 W

17. A windmill may be used to raise water from a well. A windmill raises 200 kg of water every day. The depth of the well is 5 m. What is the useful power extracted from the wind? (Given, $g = 10$ N/kg)

(a) 0.50 W (b) 0.42 W
(c) 0.32 W (d) 0.115 W

18. An athlete keeps himself fit by doing push ups.

He applies a force of 300 N as he pushes up to a distance of 0.5 m. He does 10 push ups in 30 s. What is the average power output in 30 s?

(a) 5 W
(b) 50 W
(c) 150 W
(d) 1500 W

2 Marks Questions

19. A plot of velocity *versus* time is shown in figure. A single force acts on the body.

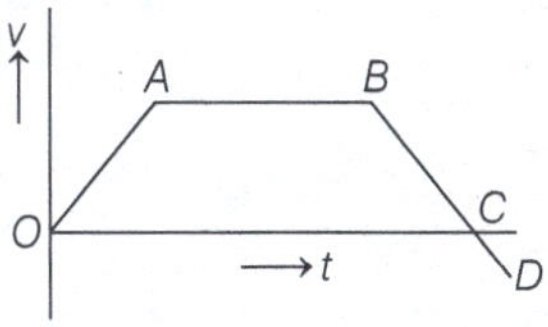

Which of them is/are not correct statements?

I. In moving from C to D, work done by the force on the body is positive.

II. In moving from B to C, work done by the force on the body is positive.

III. In moving from A to B, the body does work on the system.

IV. In moving from O to A, work is done by the body and is negative.

Codes

(a) II, III and IV (b) I, II and IV

(c) I, III and IV (d) All are incorrect

20. State [T] for True or [F] for False.

I. A boy carrying a box on his head is walking on a level road from one place to another on a straight road is doing no work.

II. When a cyclist moves on the road, work done by the road on the cycle is positive.

III. Work done is equal to area under the force-displacement graph.

IV. $1 \text{ eV} = 1.6 \times 10^{-19}$ J

Codes

	I	II	III	IV		I	II	III	IV
(a)	T	T	F	T	(b)	T	F	T	T
(c)	T	F	F	T	(d)	T	F	T	F

21. A block of mass 20 kg is pulled over a smooth inclined plane through 3 m as shown in the figure. The plane makes an angle of 30° with the base. Force applied is parallel to the base.

Assuming that no energy is lost otherwise, what is the gain in the PE of the block?

(Given, $g = 10 \text{ ms}^{-2}$)

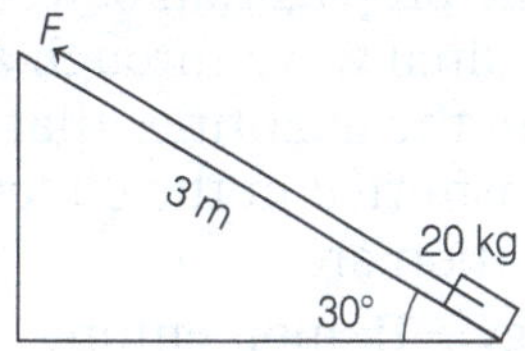

(a) 30 J (b) 20 J

(c) 300 J (d) 600 J

22. State [T] for True or [F] for False.

I. A battery converts mechanical energy into electrical energy.

II. A fish swimming in water possess mechanical energy.

III. The decrease in the PE of a ball of mass 20 kg which falls from a height 25 cm is 98 J.

IV. Potential energy is stored in a compressed spring.

V. When a car accelerates up a hill both kinetic energy and potential energy increase.

Codes

	I	II	III	IV	V
(a)	T	T	F	T	T
(b)	T	F	T	T	T
(c)	F	T	F	T	F
(d)	T	F	T	F	T

Chapter 11

Sound

1 Mark Questions

1. With the propagation of a longitudinal wave through a material medium the quantities that does not get transmitted in the direction of propagation are

I. energy II. momentum III. mass

Choose the correct option.

(a) I and II (b) I and III
(c) II and III (d) Only III

2. A sitar player plucks the wire of a sitar. After a short time each part of the wire starts vibrating in a direction perpendicular to the wire. Is the propagation of this disturbance a longitudinal or a transverse wave?

(a) Longitudinal (b) Transverse
(c) Light wave
(d) Both longitudinal and transverse

3. When a sound wave travels through a medium, the particles of the medium simply vibrate about their rest positions and do not travel from one place to another place in the medium. Which set of information about sound waves is correct?

	Nature of wave	Speed in glass (m/s)
(a)	Longitudinal	5000
(b)	Longitudinal	300000000
(c)	Transverse	5000
(d)	Transverse	300000000

4. Which of the following is not an elastic wave?

I. Sound waves II. Light waves
III. X-rays IV. Radio waves

Codes

(a) Only I
(b) II and III
(c) II, III and IV
(d) All are correct

5. Which of the following correctly describe the nature of sound, light and radiowaves?

	Sound	Light	Radio
(a)	Longitudinal	transverse	longitudinal
(b)	Longitudinal	transverse	transverse
(c)	Transverse	longitudinal	longitudinal
(d)	Transverse	longitudinal	transverse

6. A vibrating body

I. will always produce sound

II. may or may not produce sound if the amplitude of vibration is low

III. will produce sound which depend upon frequency

Choose the correct option.

(a) I and II
(b) II and III
(c) Only I
(d) Only III

7. Given waves are either transverse or longitudinal.

A. Ultrasonic waves
B. Infrasonic waves
C. X-rays
D. Waves on a string
E. Gamma rays

Group I – Transverse
Group II – Longitudinal wave

Choose the correct match.

	Group I	**Group II**
(a)	A, B	C, D, E
(b)	C, D, E	A, B
(c)	C, D	A, B, E
(d)	A, B, E	C, D

8. Given below is a diagram showing a set of percussion instruments (i.e. producing sound on being struck)

Which of the following statements is not true about the percussion instrument?

(a) The surface of the instrument vibrates when struck, thus producing sound
(b) Louder sound can be produced if hit with greater force
(c) When the vibrating surface is touched, then sound will stop
(d) These instruments can produce only loud sounds

9. Which of the following properties of sound are unaffected by change in the air temperature?

I. Frequency II. Amplitude
III. Intensity IV. Wavelength

Codes

(a) I, II and III (b) II, III and IV
(c) I, III and IV (d) II and III

10. In a recorder, the air particles in the column of air produce sound.

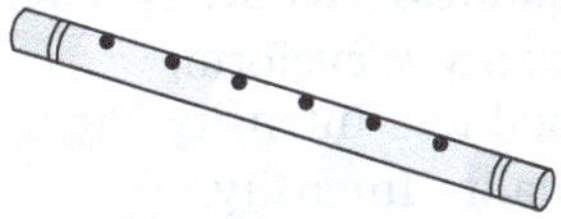

Sound is not produced when

I. all the holes are close.
II. all the holes are open.
III. one or two holes are close and one others are open.
IV. one or two holes are open.

Choose the correct option.

(a) I and II
(b) III and IV
(c) I, II and III
(d) I, II and IV

11. A trumpet and a flute are played by two students. The note from the trumpet is louder and has a lower pitch than the note from the flute. How do the amplitude and frequency of the sound from the trumpet vary compared to the amplitude and frequency from the flute?

	Trumpet's amplitude	**Trumpet's frequency**
(a)	Larger	higher
(b)	Larger	lower
(c)	Smaller	higher
(d)	Smaller	lower

12. Each of the properties of sound wave listed in Column I primarily depends on one of the quantities in Column II.

Column I	**Column II**
Quality	Intensity
Loundness	Waveform
Pitch	Frequency

Choose the matching pairs from two columns.

(a) Quality-Frequency, Loudness-Intensity, Pitch-Waveform

(b) Quality-Waveform, Loudness-Frequency, Pitch-Intensity

(c) Quality-Waveform, Loudness-Intensity, Pitch-Frequency

(d) Quality-Intensity, Loudness-Frequency, Pitch-Waveform

13. Which of the following statement is not correct?

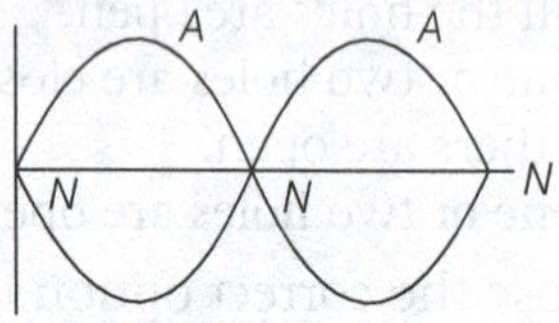

I. All nodes are in the same phase and differ from the next antinode by a path difference of $\lambda/4$.

II. All antinodes are in the same phase and differ from the immediate node by a distance of $\lambda/4$.

III. Consecutive nodes and antinodes are separated by a distance of $\lambda/2$.

Codes

(a) I and II (b) II and III

(c) I and III (d) All are correct

14. Which line on the diagram best represents the range of frequencies of sound that can be heard by a healthy human ear?

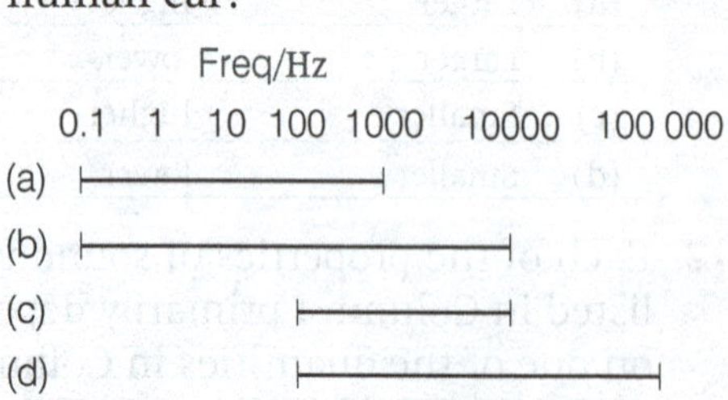

15. Ultrasonic waves can be produced using

I. Galton whistle

II. piezoelectric oscillator

III. magnetostriction

Codes

(a) I and II

(b) II and III

(c) I and III

(d) I, II and III

16. A sonic tape measure is used to measure the length of a room. It measures a time interval of 0.060 s between transmitting a sound pulse and receiving the echo. The speed of sound in air is 330 m/s. How far is the reflecting wall from the tape measure?

(a) 5.5 m (b) 9.9 m

(c) 11 m (d) 20 m

17. A sound wave is reflected from a brick wall. Compared with the incident wave, the reflected wave has

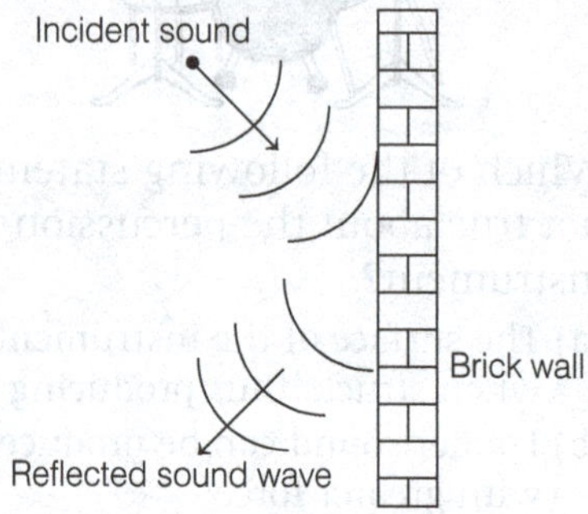

(a) a greater amplitude

(b) a shorter wavelength

(c) the same speed

(d) the same velocity

2 Marks Questions

18. The diagram below shows a boy and a girl attempting to find out details about the on-coming train.

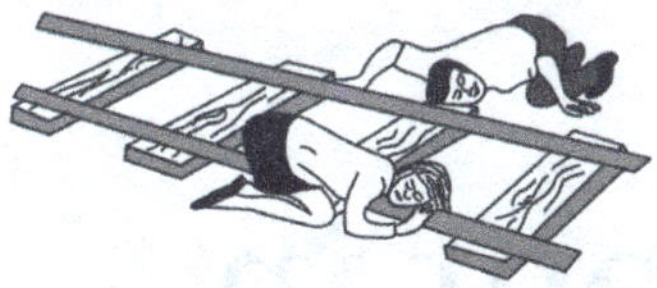

Which of the following statements is not true about the given picture?

I. Railway tracks always produce soft sound when we hear.

II. Sound waves travel faster in solids than in air.

III. The sound they hear on tracks were produced by the vibrating air particles.

Codes

(a) I and III (b) Only I

(c) I, II and III (d) I and III

19. Read the following statements.

I. Velocity of sound changes with increase of humidity of air.

II. Velocity of sound remains unchanged with change of temperature of medium.

III. A sound wave is passing through air column in the form of compression and rarefaction. In consecutive compressions and rarefactions, there is no transfer of heat.

Choose the correct statements from the options given below.

(a) I and II (b) II and III

(c) III and I (d) I, II and III

20. Which of the following statement(s) is/are correct?

I. Waves produced in a cylinder containing a liquid by moving its piston back and forth are longitudinal waves.

II. In longitudinal waves, the particle of the medium oscillate perpendicular to the direction of propagation of the wave.

III. The longitudinal waves are called pressure waves.

IV. Propagation of longitudinal waves through a medium involves change in pressure and volume of air when compression and rarefaction are formed.

Codes

(a) Only I

(b) Only II

(c) I, II and IV

(d) I, III and IV

21. Match the Column I with Column II.

	Column I		Column II
A.	String vibration	1.	Tabla
B.	Membrane vibration	2.	Bicycle bell
C.	Vibration of air column	3.	Sitar
D.	Vibration of plate	4.	Flute

Codes

	A	B	C	D		A	B	C	D
(a)	1	4	2	3	(b)	3	1	4	2
(c)	4	2	3	1	(d)	2	3	1	4

22. An oil-tanker explodes in the sea. At that instant an aircraft and a submarine were present vertically above and below the oil-tanker respectively at equal distances from it. Find the ratio of the time taken by sound waves to reach them.

(Speed of sound in air = 340 m/s.

Speed of sound in sea water = 1520 m/s)

(a) 5.40 (b) 4.47 (c) 5.57 (d) 6.40

Chapter

12

Improvement in Food Resources

1 Mark Questions

1. Salman had grown wheat crops in his field. After few months, he observed brown colour rust in wheat crops. What could be the causal agent of it?

(a) Soil
(b) Seed
(c) Air
(d) Water

2. Ram had a plot just behind the bank of a river. Each time he planted kharif crop, the crop got damaged due to floods. He consulted the agricultural scientist who gave him a special variety of seeds and also advised him to practice fish farming. What was the speciality of seed grains?

(a) Paddy seeds
(b) Wheat seeds
(c) Corn sees
(d) Paddy and wheat seeds

3. Match the following columns and write the complete sentences giving one additional information about the sentence.

Column I	Column II
A. Black gram	1. are grown from November-April
B. Rabi crops	2. is a farming system with minimal or no use of chemical and maximum input of organic manure.
C. Nitrogen, phosphorus, potassium, calcium magnesium and sulphur	3. include insecticides, herbicides and fungicides.
D. Organic farming	4. is a protein yielding pulse.
E. Pesticides	5. are all macronutrients

Codes

	A	B	C	D		A	B	C	D
(a)	2	3	1	2	(b)	1	2	3	4
(c)	4	1	2	3	(d)	3	2	1	4

4. Refer to the given Venn diagram.

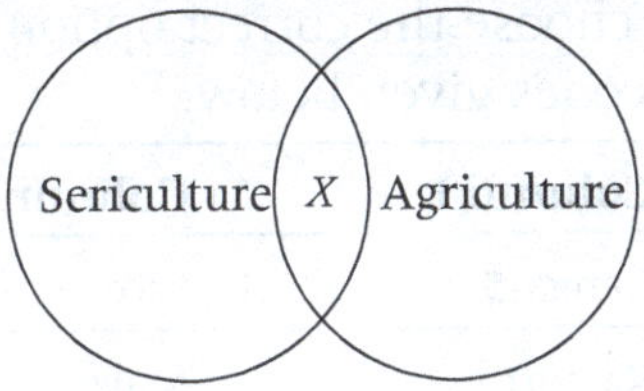

Choose the correct option for X.

(a) Crop rotation (b) Mixed farming
(c) Inter cropping (d) Integrated farming

5. Ankit went to his village in summer vacation. He wanted to help his father in farming, so he did excessive irrigation in the field.

Choose the possible outcomes of the excessive irrigation done by Ankit.

I. Water logging.
II. Increase salinity.
III. Weakening of roots of crops.
IV. Soil erosion.

Codes

(a) I, II and IV (b) Only I
(c) Only III (d) All of these

6. Given below are four statement regarding improvement in food resources. Choose the false statement from the options given below.

I. Farming without use of chemicals as fertilisers, herbicides and pesticides is known as organic farming.
II. Growing of wheat and groundnut on the same field is called crop rotation.
III. *Xanthium* and *Parthenium* are commonly known as weeds.
IV. Planting soybean and maize in alternate rows in the same field is called intercropping.

Codes

(a) I and IV (b) II and III
(c) Only II (d) III and IV

7. Refer to the given Venn diagram.

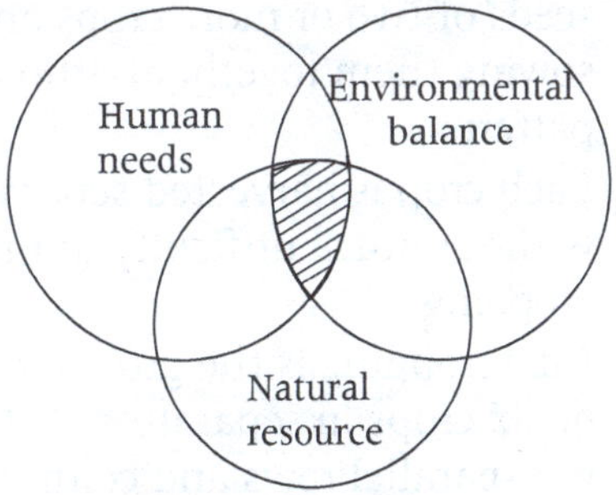

Choose the most suitable option for shaded region.

(a) Organic farming
(b) Sustainable agriculture
(c) Modern farming
(d) Vermicomposting

8. Given below picture represents the agricultural field in which crops are grown. Observe the picture and find the cropping pattern.

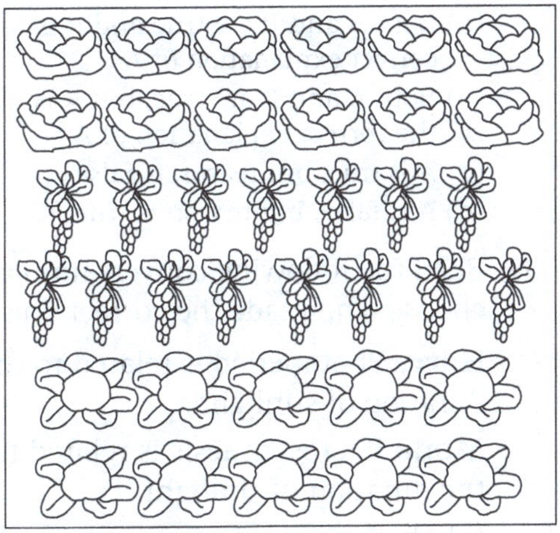

(a) Mixed cropping
(b) Intercropping
(c) Monocropping
(d) None of the above

9. Consider the following statements and choose the correct answer from the options given below.

I. Mixed cropping is the mixing of seeds of two or more crops and sowing them together without any pattern.

II. Each crop is harvested separately without much difficulty in mixed cropping.

III. Intercropping is the growing of five or six crops in separate non-parallel rows and columns.

IV. Wheat and gram are the samples of mixed cropping.

Codes

(a) I, II and III (b) I and IV

(c) I, II and IV (d) Only IV

10. **Assertion** (A) *A. mellifera*, an exotic bee species is commercially employed in apiaries.

Reason (R) It produces high yield of honey.

(a) Both A and R are true and R is the correct explanation of A

(b) Both A and R are true, but R is not the correct explanation of A

(c) A is true, but reason is false

(d) A is false, but reason is true

11. Read the following conversation and choose who made the correct one.

Harry Photoperiod is related to the duration of sunlight.

Mona Photosynthesis is related to the duration of sunlight.

(a) Mona

(b) Harry

(c) Both of them

(d) None of them

12. Match the Column I with Column II and choose the correct option from the codes given below.

Column I	Column II
A. Ganga-5	1. Rice
B. Kasturi	2. Maize
C. Green manure	3. Brown-Swiss
D. Exotic breed	4. Biofertiliser

Codes

	A	B	C	D		A	B	C	D
(a)	1	3	2	4	(b)	2	1	4	3
(c)	4	3	1	2	(d)	4	2	1	3

13. Refer to the given Venn diagram.

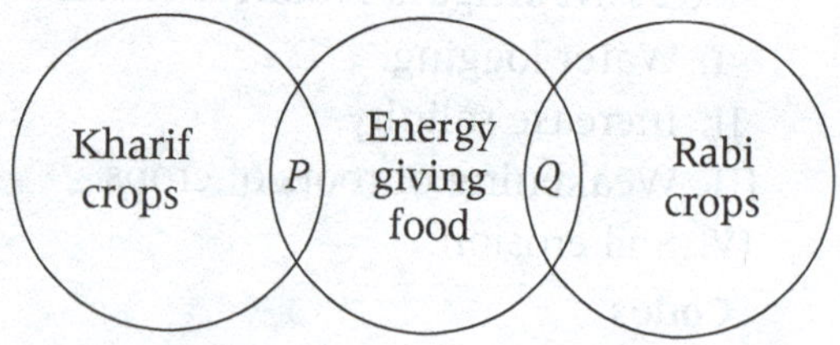

Choose the correct option for *P* and *Q*.

	P	*Q*
(a)	Wheat	Maize
(b)	Gram	Soybean
(c)	Maize	Wheat
(d)	Mustard	Maize

14. Refer to the Venn diagram and

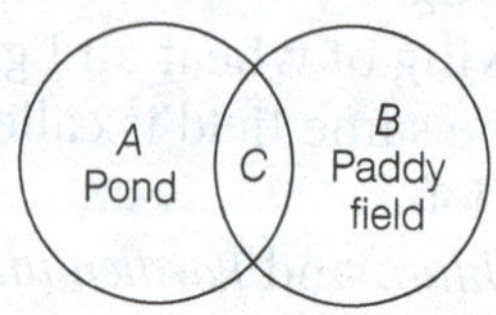

choose the correct option for *C*.

(a) Apiculture (b) Aquaculture

(c) Poultry farming (d) Pisciculture

15. "Seeds" in fish farming refers to
(a) eggs (b) food
(c) larvae (d) female adult fish

16. **Assertion** (A) Large schools of fish are located using radio signals.
Reason (R) Radio signals help in increasing the fish yield.
(a) Both A and R are true and R is the correct explanation of A
(b) Both A and R are true, but R is not the correct explanation of A
(c) A is true, R is false
(d) Both A and R are false

17. Refer to the given Venn diagram and select the missing nutrient.

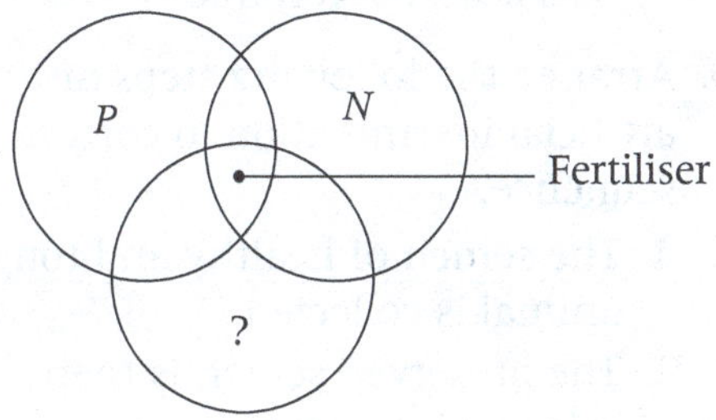

(a) Fe (b) Cl (c) K (d) Mg

18. Cattle feed includes roughage and concentrates which are .... and .... , respectively.
(a) largely fibre; rich in protein level
(b) largely proteins; high in fibre
(c) low in fibre; low in nutrients
(d) largely proteins ; low in nutrients

19. In cattle farming, a person want to increase production of milk, so he made cross-breed '*X*' with '*Y*' animal. Out of which '*X*' is a foreign breed. Choose the correct option for '*X*' and '*Y*'.
(a) *X* is selected for excellent resistance to disease
(b) *Y* is an exotic breed
(c) *X* is selected for long lactation periods
(d) *Y* is selected for long lactation period

20. Raghu's father had two healthy Sahiwal cows. Raghu told that the lactation period of cows can be increased by cross-breeding cattle with foreign breeds and also it was possible artificially. In this way if villagers participated in cross-breeding they would have higher milk yield. What is meant by lactation period?
(a) It is period of milk production before birth of a young one lasting generally upto next pregnancy
(b) It is period from birth to death of cow
(c) It is period of milk production after birth of a young one lasting generally upto next pregnancy
(d) None of the above

21. **Assertion** (A) Dr. V Kurien is known as the father of white revolution.
Reason (R) White revolution is associated with milk production.
(a) Both A and R are true and R is the correct explanation of A
(b) Both A and R are true, but R is not the correct explanation of A
(c) A is true, but R is false
(d) A is false, but R is true

22. **Assertion** (A) Honeybees are nuisance to farmer.
Reason (R) Bees destroy the crops to fulfill their nutritional requirements.
(a) Both A and R are true and R is a correct explanation of A
(b) Both A and R are true, but R is not a correct explanation of A
(c) A is true, but R is false
(d) Both A and R are false

23. Choose the correct pair of vitamins that is kept high in the poultry feeds.
(a) Vitamin-A and C (b) Vitamin-B and K
(c) Vitamin-A and K (d) Vitamin-A and C

24.

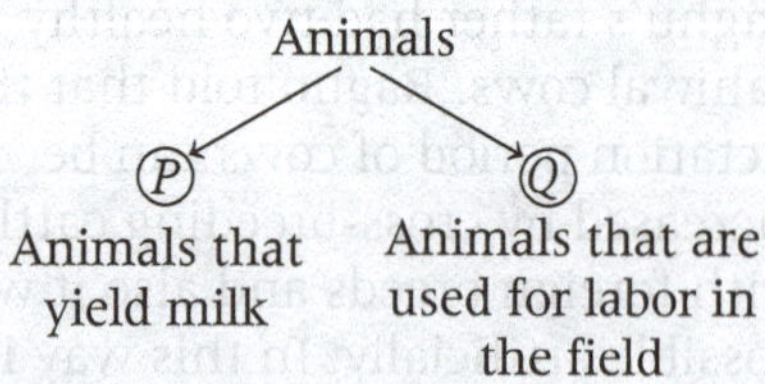

Choose the correct option for *P* and *Q*.

	P	*Q*
(a)	Milch animal	Drought animal
(b)	GMO	Milch animal
(c)	Drought animal	Milch animal
(d)	Animal husbandry	GMO

25. **Assertion** (A) Inspite of large population of catte, milk production is meagre in India.

Reason (R) Poor quality feed is given to cattle.

(a) Both A and R are true and R is the correct explanation of A
(b) Both A and R are true, but R is not the correct explanation of A
(c) A is true, but R is false
(d) Both A and R are false

26.

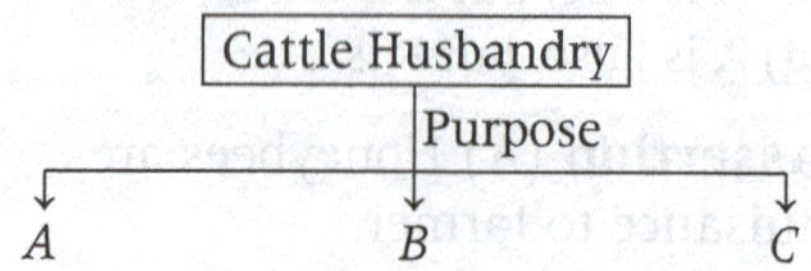

Choose the correct option for *A*, *B* and *C*.

	A	*B*	*C*
(a)	Milk production	Egg production	Meat production
(b)	Milk production	Meat production	Fish production
(c)	Meat production	Milk production	Agricultural work
(d)	Meat production	Fish production	Agricultural work

27. Silver revolution is related to the increase in the production of

(a) meat (b) wool (c) milk (d) egg

28. **Assertion** (A) Pesticides are harmful for living organisms and cause environmental pollution.

Reason (R) Organic farming is environment-friendly and does not rely much on agricultural chemicals.

(a) Both A and R are true and R is the correct explanation of A
(b) Both A and R are true, but R is not the correct explanation of A
(c) A is true, but R is false
(d) A is false, but R is true

29. Arrange the following steps of artificial insemination in correct sequence.

I. The semen of healthy and tough animal is collected.
II. The preserved semen is then injected into genetical tract of female animals.
III. It is preserved by freezing or chemical methods.

Codes

(a) I → II → III (b) II → I → III
(c) III → I → II (d) I → III → II

30. Match the Column I with Column II.

Column I	Column II
A. Mericulture	1. Catching fish from natural resources.
B. Aquaculture	2. Culture of marine fishes for commercial use.
C. Capture fishing	3. Cultivation of aquatic products under controlled condition.
D. Apiculture	4. Culturing of honeybee for product of honey and wax.

Codes

	A	B	C	D		A	B	C	D
(a)	2	1	3	4	(b)	2	3	1	4
(c)	3	1	2	4	(d)	2	1	3	4

31. Which crop can be a part of fish culture?

(a) Wheat (b) Maize
(c) Barley (d) Paddy

2 Marks Questions

32. Match the Column I with Column II.

Column I	Column II
A. Green revolution	1. Milk
B. Yellow revolution	2. Fish
C. Blue revolution	3. Food grains
D. White revolution	4. Oil
E. Golden revolution	5. Wheat
	6. Pulses

Codes

	A	B	C	D	E
(a)	2	1	4	5	3
(b)	3	4	2	1	5
(c)	3	4	2	1	6
(d)	5	4	2	1	6

33. Match the Column I with Column II.

Column I	Column II
A. Magnesium	1. Weed
B. Pathogens	2. Hybrid
C. Cross breeding	3. Macronutrient
D. Compost	4. Disease causing organisms
E. Cyperinus	5. Animal refuse

Codes

	A	B	C	D	E
(a)	2	1	3	4	5
(b)	1	2	3	4	5
(c)	3	4	2	5	1
(d)	5	4	2	2	1

34. The daily food requirement or the ration for broilers is

(a) carbohydrate rich with adequate minerals
(b) protein rich diet with adequate fat
(c) fat rich with adequate carbohydrates
(d) Carbohydrate rich with adequate fat

35. State [T] for True and [F] for False.

I. Vermicomposting is better than composting.
II. The housing, nutritional and environmental requirement of broilers and layers are same.
III. Fertilisers have more amount of nutrients than manure.
IV. Anthrax is a bacterial disease that is transmitted from animals to humans.

Codes

	I	II	III	IV		I	II	III	IV
(a)	T	F	T	T	(b)	F	F	F	T
(c)	T	T	T	F	(d)	F	T	F	F

36. Match the Column I with Column II.

Column I	Column II
A. Catla	1. Bottom feeder
B. Rohu	2. Surface feeder
C. Mrigal	3. Central zone feeder
D. Pisciculture	4. Culture fishery

Codes

	A	B	C	D
(a)	4	3	2	1
(b)	2	3	1	4
(c)	2	3	4	1
(d)	2	1	3	4

37. Categorize the following animals into exotic and local/indigenous breeds.

P-Brown Swiss　*R*-Aseel
T-Red Sindhi　*Q*-Jersey
S-Leghorn　*U*-Sahiwal

Codes

	Exotic	Local
(a)	*P, Q, R*	*S, T, U*
(b)	*P, U, S*	*Q, R, T*
(c)	*P, S, Q*	*R, T, U*
(d)	*Q, R, T*	*P, S, U*

38. Choose the correct option for percent of protein content in milk, egg and fish, respectively.
(a) 3.5%, 19%, 13%　(b) 13%, 19%, 4%
(c) 4%, 13%, 19%　(d) 10%, 15%, 2%

39. **Assertion** (A) Fumigation is done in cattle farming.
Reason (R) Fumigation using chemicals can kill pests.
(a) Both A and R are true and R is the correct explanation of A
(b) Both A and R are true, but R is not the correct explanation of A
(c) A is true, but R is false
(d) A is false, but R is true

40. Match the Column I with Column II.

Column I	Column II
A. *Parthenium*	1. Liver
B. Flukes	2. Eggs
C. Layers	3. The rock bee
D. *A. dorsata*	4. The little bee
E. *A. florae*	5. Gajar ghas

Codes

	A	B	C	D	E
(a)	1	3	5	2	4
(b)	1	5	2	4	3
(c)	5	1	3	4	2
(d)	5	1	2	4	3

PRACTICE SET 01

1 Mark Questions

1. A car moving with a uniform speed covers a distance of 120 m in 2 s. What time will it take to cover 240 m?
   (a) 1 s (b) 2 s
   (c) 3 s (d) 4 s

2. Simple epethelium is a tissue in which cells are
   (a) hardened and provide to organs
   (b) continuously dividing to provide to form an organ
   (c) cemented directly to one another to form a single layer
   (d) loosely connceted to one another to form an irregular layer

3. In which of the following compounds, the valency of each of the constituent elements is equal to the total number of atoms in one molecule of the compound?
   (a) HCl
   (b) H_2S
   (c) CaO
   (d) $MgCl_2$

4. The body will float in equilibrium, if
   I. centre of gravity and centre of buoyancy lie along the same line.
   II. weight of body is equal to weight of liquid displaced by sinking part of body.
   III. centre of buoyancy coincides with the centre of gravity.
   IV. weight of body is equal to weight of the liquid displaced by whole volume of the body.

   Which of the given conditions is true?
   (a) I and II
   (b) III and IV
   (c) I, II and III
   (d) I, III and IV

5. The ratio of the radii of hydrogen atom and its nucleus is $\sim 10^5$. Assume that the atom and the nucleus are spherical. If atom is represented by planet Earth with radius 6.4×10^6 m, then the size of the nucleus will be
   (a) 8 m (b) 10 m
   (c) 10^5 m (d) 64 m

6. Match the Column I with Column II.

	Column I		Column II
A.	$1\ Nm^{-2}$	1.	10^{-5} bar
B.	1 g wt.	2.	10 dyne cm^{-2}
C.	1 Pa	3.	10 Pa
D.	$1\ kg\text{-}fm^{-2}$	4.	980 dyne

	A	B	C	D
(a)	1	2	3	4
(b)	2	4	1	3
(c)	4	3	2	1
(d)	4	1	2	3

7. To avoid bends as well as the toxic effects of high concentration of nitrogen in the blood, scuba divers used the tanks filled with air having
   (a) 32% O_2 and remaining He
   (b) 32% N_2 and 56% O_2
   (c) 72% O_2 and 11% He
   (d) 56% N_2, 32% O_2 and 11% He

8. What properties should be a material have in order to be suitable as a heat shield?

	Its melting point must be	It must conduct heat
(a)	Higher than that of the space capsule	Well
(b)	Higher than that of the space capsule	Poorly
(c)	Lower than that of the space capsule	Well
(d)	Lower than that of the space capsule	Poorly

9. Palki takes nitrogen and hydrogen combine together to form ammonia.

$$N_2 + 3H_2 \longrightarrow 2NH_3$$

[Relative atomic masses of N = 1u, H = 1u]

The mass of nitrogen and hydrogen which combine together to form 6.8 g ammonia is

(a) N_2= 2.8g, H_2= 4.0 g
(b) N_2 = 5.6 g, H_2= 1.2 g
(c) N_2 = 4.0 g, H_2= 2.8 g
(d) N_2 = 1.2 g, H_2= 5.6 g

10. Which of the following craps would require a miniumu quantity of NPK or urea dor their proper growth?

(a) Paddy
(b) Peas
(c) Wheat
(d) Groundnut

11. The diagrams show the same object on a smooth table. Four different pairs of forces act on the object. Which pair of forces causes to greatest acceleration?

(a) 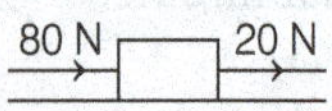

(b) 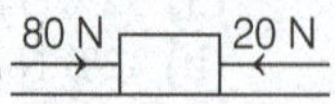

(c) 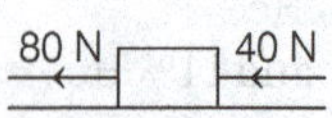

(d) 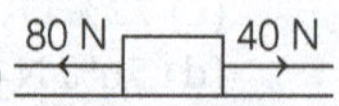

12. Two particles X and Y have the composition shown in the given table.

Particle	Number of electron	Number of neutron	Number of proton
X	10	8	8
Y	18	18	17

The particles X and Y are

(a) metal atoms
(b) non-metal atoms
(c) neutral atoms
(d) positive ions

13. Radha, bought grapes and she kept them in water to remove dirt. But unfortunately, she forgst to remove water from the bowl. After 24 hour, she observed that grapes sweel up. Which of the following option correctly describes above situation?

(a) Solution is hypotonic
(b) Solution is more concentrated are hypertonic
(c) Grapes are having concentrated cell sap
(d) All of the above

14. A 56 inches LED television of mass 5 kg is lifted by four men to a height of 1 m. They hold it without raising or lowering it. How much work is done by them in lifting the box?

(a) 50 J (b) 5000 J
(c) 50 kJ (d) 500 J

15. Which sulphide contains the greatest mass of sulphur in a 10 g sample?

Sulphide	Formula	Mass of one mol/g
A	NiS	90
B	FeS_2	120
C	MoS_2	160
D	PbS	239

(a) A (b) B (c) C (d) D

16. A patient is diagnosed with a viral infection. Which of the following treatments has the highest chance of being effective?

(a) Penicillin (b) Deoxycycline
(c) Tetracycline (d) None of these

17. A train is running at a speed of 90 km/h. It crosses a bridge of 600 m in 1 min. What would be the length of the train?

(a) 900 m (b) 1200 m
(c) 1500 m (d) 1800 m

18. Complete the diagram to show how a muscle cell gets its energy? Choose the correct option from options below.

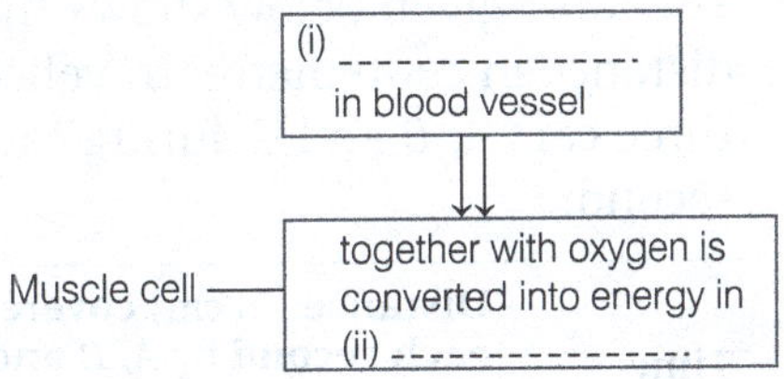

	(i)	(ii)
(a)	digested food	cytoplasm
(b)	blood	cell sap
(c)	blood	cytoplasm
(d)	cytoplasm	cell sap

19. Ablative protection is not used on the nose cones of passenger aircraft. What is the reason for this?

(a) The heat shields are too heavy to carry on passenger aircraft
(b) Passenger aircraft fly at an altitude where the air is more dense
(c) There is a great difference in speed between spacecraft and aircraft
(d) The heat shield would disturb the aerodynamics of the passenger aircraft

20. The subatomic particle which is not present in the nucleus and directs the properties of elements is/are

(a) electron (b) neutron
(c) proton and neutron (d) proton

21. A goal keeper in a game of football pulls his hands backwards after holding the ball shot at the goal. This enables the goal keeper to

(a) exert larger force on the ball
(b) reduce the force exerted by the ball on hands
(c) increase the rate of change of momentum
(d) decrease the rate of change of momentum

22. Intestine absorb the digested food particles. What type of epithelial cells are responsible for that?

(a) Stratified squamous epithelium
(b) Columnar epithelium
(c) Spindle fibrous
(d) Cuboidal epithelium

23. A submarine is a water craft capable of independent operation underwater. A small submarine of mass 1000 kg sinks in water with a uniform speed of 2 m/s. What is the resultant force exerted on the submarine as it sinks?

(a) 0 (b) 500 N
(c) 2000 N (d) 10,000 N

24. A small amount of the sample of a soil was mixed with water in beaker. After stirring for some time, the beaker was allowed to stand. The mud was found to settle down. The liquid above the mud was carefully filtered. The filtrate will be

(a) a true solution (b) a colloidal solution
(c) a suspension (d) Both (a) and (b)

25. Study the concept map below.

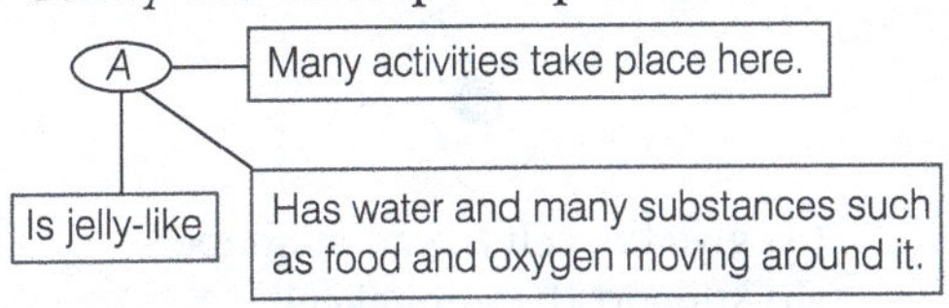

A is the ....

(a) cell membrane (b) cytoplasm
(c) chloroplast (d) nucleus

26. A windmill may be used to raise water from a well. It raises 180 kg of water every hour. The dept of well is 6 m. What is the useful power extracted from the wind?

(a) 9 W (b) 6 W
(c) 3 W (d) 12 W

27. State [T] for True and (F) for False.

I. Cooking of vegetables is a chemical change.
II. Boiling of water is a physical change.
III. Cutting of fruits is a chemical change
IV. Twinkling of stars is a chemical change.

Codes

	I	II	III	IV		I	II	III	IV
(a)	T	T	F	F	(b)	F	F	T	T
(c)	T	F	T	F	(d)	T	F	F	T

28. A mechanical wave propagates in a medium along the direction of wave propagation as shown. The particles of the medium

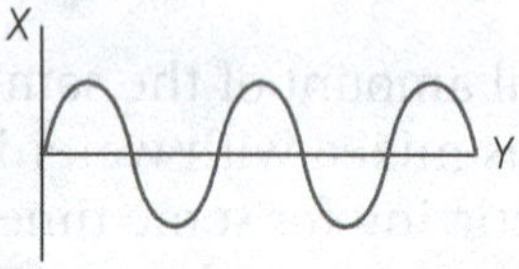

(a) move in Y-axis
(b) move in X-axis
(c) can move in either X-axis or Y-axis
(d) cannot move in either axis

29. The diagram below shows a typical animal cell. The function of Y is to ....

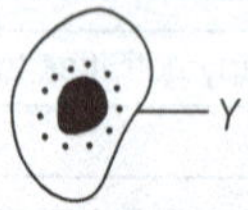

(a) give the cell a regular shape
(b) support the animal cell
(c) control the movement of substances in and out of the cell
(d) contain new substances

30. A motor pumps out the underground water. A motor pump of power 2 kW is used to raise water to a height of 20 m. How much water per minute will be raised?

(a) 1200 kg (b) 600 kg
(c) 1000 kg (d) 300 kg

31. Consider the following ionic species.

I. Fluoride ion II. Aluminium ion
III. Oxide ion IV. Sodium ion

Which of the following has more electrons than neutrons?

(a) I and II (b) II and IV
(c) Only III (d) Only II

32. The table given below shows the distance in centemetre, travelled by three cars *A*, *B* and *C* during each second.

Time	**Distance** (in cm) **covered in each second by *A*, *B* and *C***		
	Car *A*	**Car *B***	**Car *C***
1st second	20	20	20
2nd second	20	36	60
3rd second	20	24	100
4th second	20	30	140
5th second	20	48	180

Which car is moving with a non-uniform acceleration?

(a) *A* (b) *B*
(c) *C* (d) None of these

33. When plant cells are observed after staining them with iodine solution, some parts are usually stained dark blue or purple. When animal cells are stained with the solution, there is no part of the cell that will be stained dark blue or purple. What does this experiment tell you?

(a) Animal cells have parts that contain starch
(b) Plant cells usually have parts that contain starch
(c) Animal cells allow iodine to get into them but plant cells do not
(d) Plant cells allow iodine solution to get into them but animal cells do not

34. The diagram given below shows the process of osmosis.

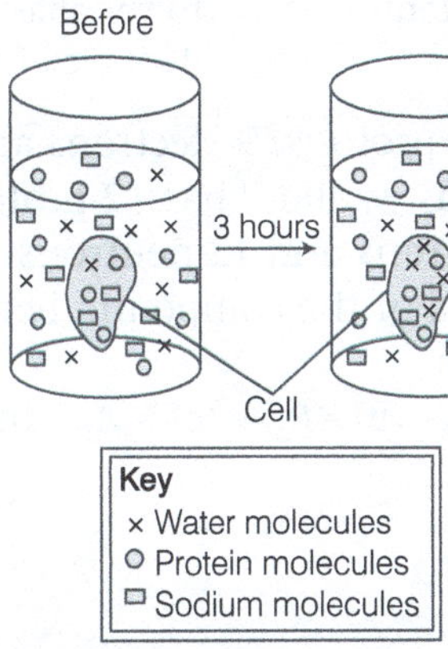

Diffusion of a solvent through a semipermeable membrane from a region of low solute concentration to a region of high solute concentration is known as osmosis. In the above diagram, which molecule is showing the process of osmosis?

(a) Sodium molecule (b) Protein molecule
(c) Water molecule (d) All of these

35. The speed of sound in air is about 344 m/s and speed of light in air is 3×10^8 m/s. It is thus clear that the speed of light is very great as compared to speed of sound. So, though sound may take a few seconds to travel a distance of a few hundred metres, light will take practically no time to reach a distance of even a few kilometres.

Sound of thunderstorm is heard 10 s after the lightning is seen. The approximate distance of the thunder cloud is

(a) 3.4 m (b) 3.44 km
(c) 30.4 km (d) 340 km

36. What is the difference between Cell *A* and Cell *B* ?

Cell *A*	**Cell *B***
Has two membranes	Has only one membrane
Can make its own food	Cannot make its own food
Has *Y* that allows gaseous exchange	Has no *Y*
Has a fixed rectangular shape	Has a fixed round shape

(a) Cell *A* is a plant cell and *B* is animal cell
(b) Cell *B* is a plant cell and *A* is animal cell
(c) Both *A* and *B* are plant cell
(d) Both *A* and *B* are animal cell

37. Which of the following sound waves shown in the figure represent sounds of the same loudness but different pitch?

I. II. III. IV.

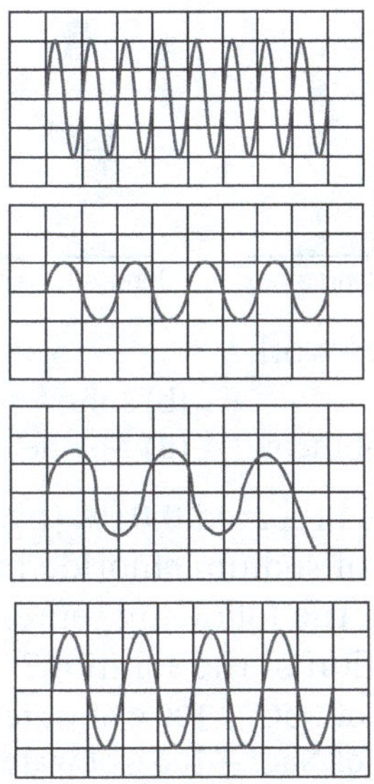

(a) Both I and II (b) Both II and III
(c) Both I and IV (d) Both II and IV

38. Observe the following flow chart.

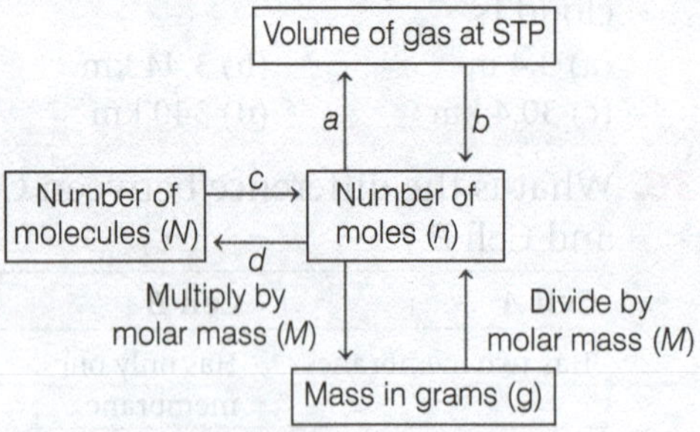

Consider the following statements.

I. a = multiply by 22.4 L, b = divide by 22.4 L

II. c = multiply by N_A, d = divide by N_A

III. a = divide by 22.4 L, b = multiply by 22.4 L

IV. c = divide by N_A, d = multiply by N_A

The correct statements are

(a) I and II (b) I and IV
(c) II and III (d) III and IV

39. Velocity-time graph for a moving object is found to be curved line, then its acceleration is

(a) constant (b) variable
(c) zero (d) None of these

40. A has 9 protons, 9 electrons and 10 neutrons, while B has 12 protons, 12 electrons and 12 neutrons. Formula of the compound between A and B is

(a) BA_2 (b) AB_2 (c) B_2A_3 (d) AB_4

2 Marks Questions

41. The diagram below shows two different situations.

Peter is lifting a box. John is holding a box.

Who does work?

(a) Peter (b) John
(c) Both of them (d) No one

42. Arun has prepared 0.01% (by mass) solution of sodium chloride in water. Which of the following represents the composition of the solution?

(a) 1.00 g of NaCl + 100 g of water
(b) 0.11 g of NaCl + 100 g of water
(c) 0.01 g of NaCl + 99.99 g of water
(d) 0.10 g of NaCl + 99.90 g of water

43. The nucleus of both plant and animal cells contain one or more dense bodies known as nucleolus. Which of the following is correct about nucleolus?

I. It helps in formation of new DNA molecules.

II. It helps in organisation of the spindle during nuclear division.

III. It helps in replication of mitochondria following nuclear division.

IV. It facilitates formation of ribosomes.

V. It is dense, spherical and membrane-less structure.

Codes

(a) I and II (b) II and III
(c) III and IV (d) IV and V

44. Anita of mass 45 kg wears stilettos (pencil heeled shoes) which occupy an area of $1 cm^2$ by one heel. What would be the pressure exerted on the ground if she stands on just one heel ($g = 10 ms^{-2}$).

(a) 4.5×10^5 Pa

(b) 4.5×10^6 Pa

(c) 4.5×10^4 Pa

(d) 4.5×10^2 Pa

45. Select the odd one out.

(a) The movement of water across a semi-permeable membrane is affected by the amount of substances dissolved in it

(b) Membranes are made of organic molecules like proteins and lipids

(c) The cell membrane separates the content of the cell from its external environment

(d) The cell membrane allows the movement of all material across it

46. Match the Column I with Column II.

Column I	Column II
A. Protons	1. Number of positively charged particles in nucleus.
B. Carbon dating	2. Positively charged particles.
C. Valence electrons	3. Technique to know age of fossils.
D. Atomic number	4. Number of electrons in outermost shell.
	5. Age of Earth.

Codes

	A	B	C	D
(a)	1	3	4	2
(b)	2	5	4	1
(c)	2	3	4	1
(d)	3	2	1	4

47. A racing car is fitted with an electronic monitoring system. Data from the car is used to plot a speed-time graph for part of the race. The graph is displayed on a computer screen.

The graph covers a period of time when the car is first at rest, then

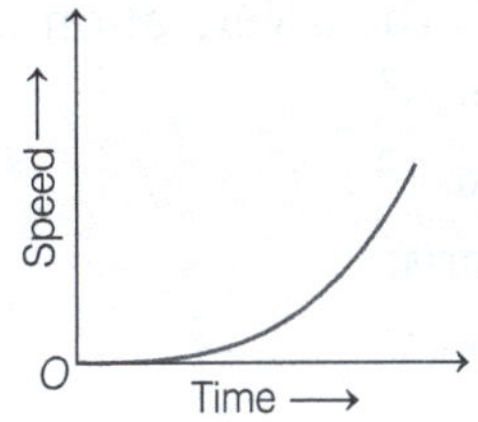

(a) moving with uniform speed and then moving with uniform acceleration

(b) moving with uniform speed and then moving with non-uniform acceleration

(c) moving with uniform acceleration and then moving with non-uniform acceleration

(d) moving with non-uniform acceleration and then moving with uniform acceleration

48. Match the Column I with those of Column II.

Column I	Column II
A. Chewing / cutting	1. Borer
B. Sucking	2. Locust
C. Boring	3. Parthenium
D. Weed	4. Aphids

Codes

	A	B	C	D
(a)	3	2	4	1
(b)	1	2	3	4
(c)	2	4	1	3
(d)	2	3	1	4

49. A car of mass 800 kg is being driven along a level road. The engine supplies a forward force of 3600 N and the total resistive force is 2000 N.

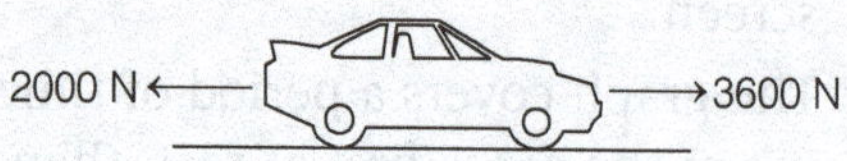

What is the acceleration of the car?

(a) 2.0 m/s^2

(b) 2.5 m/s^2

(c) 4.5 m/s^2

(d) 7.0 m/s^2

50. Read the given statements and choose the correct option.

Statement I When water is heated in a closed vessel, pressure inside the vessel increases.

Statement II Pressure is directly proportional to the volume.

Statement III The water vapours have greater kinetic energy. Thus, molecules of water vapours exert more pressure on the walls of the vessel.

Codes

(a) I and II (b) Only II

(c) I and III (d) Only III

PRACTICE SET 02

1 Mark Questions

1. A body covers 20, 22, 24 and 26 metres in 6th, 7th, 8th and 9th second, respectively. Then, which of the following conditions is true?
   (a) The body starts from rest and moves with a uniform velocity
   (b) The body starts from rest and moves with a uniform acceleration
   (c) The body starts with an initial velocity and moves with a uniform acceleration
   (d) The body starts with an initial velocity and moves with a uniform velocity

2. The letters *X*, *Y* and *Z* represent different atoms $^{40}_{19}X$, $^{39}_{19}Y$ and $^{40}_{20}Z$.
   What can be deduced from the proton numbers and nucleon numbers of *X*, *Y* and *Z*?
   (a) *X* and *Y* are the same element
   (b) *X* and *Z* are the same element
   (c) *X* has more protons than *Y*
   (d) *Z* has more neutrons than *Y*

3. Organisms without nucleus and cell organelles belong to
   I. Fungi
   II. Protista
   III. Cyanobacteria
   IV. Archaebacteria
   Choose the correct option.
   (a) I and II
   (b) III and IV
   (c) I and IV
   (d) II and III

4. **Statement I** Pressure is a vector quantity.
   Statement II Pressure depends on force which is a vector quantity.
   Which of the following statement(s) is/are correct?
   (a) Only I (b) Only II
   (c) Both I and II (d) Neither I nor II

5. Given below figure represent a cell.

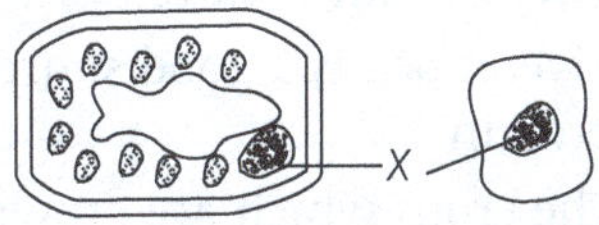

   Identify the function of *X* from the options?
   (a) To make food
   (b) To ensure that the cell has food
   (c) To protect the cell
   (d) To control the activities in the cell

6. In a sample of ethyl ethanoate ($CH_3COOC_2H_5$), the two oxygen atoms have the same number of electrons but different number of neutrons. Which of the following is the correct reason for it?
   I. One of the oxygen atoms has gained electrons.
   II. One of the oxygen atoms has gained two neutrons.
   III. The two oxygen atoms are isotopes.
   IV. The two oxygen atoms are isobars.
   Codes
   (a) I and II (b) II and III
   (c) Only III (d) I and IV

7. Work done is the product of force applied and displacement. Work done can also be calculated by graphical method. A force *versus* displacement (F-x) graph is shown in the figure. Find the total work done by the force.

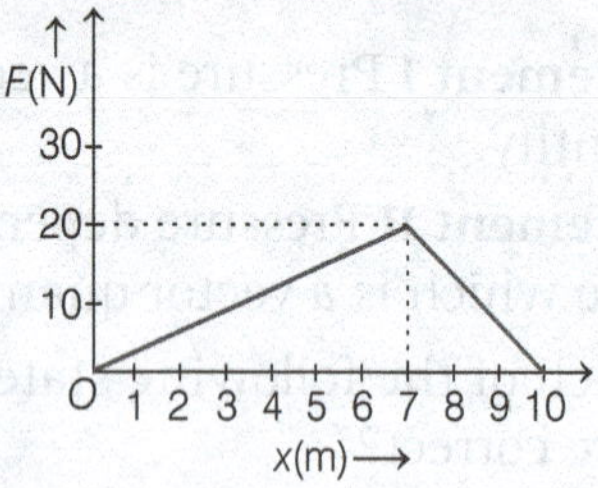

(a) 100 J (b) 90 J
(c) 80 J (d) 70 J

8. Identify the false statement.

I. Pigeon pea is a good source of protein.
II. The crops which are grown in rainy season are called Rabi crops.
III. Vegetable are rich in vitamins.
IV. Kharif crops grows in winter season.

Codes
(a) I and III (b) II and IV
(c) Only I (d) Only II

9. Rohan and Rahul made to measure the mass of their two balls by using a balance. Mass of the balls were 10 g and 20 g. Rohan then asked Rahul that what will be the ratio of kinetic energies of ball, if their momentum is same for which Rahul answered correctly. What was Rahul's answer?

(a) 1 : 2 (b) 2 : 1 (c) 1 : 4 (d) 4 : 1

10. Match the Column I with Column II.

	Column I		Column II
A.	0.25 mol oxygen	1.	N_A molecules
B.	18 g water	2.	$N_A/4$ molecules
C.	46 g Na-atom	3.	N_A atoms
D.	1 mol C-atom	4.	$N_A \times 2$ atoms

Codes

	A	B	C	D
(a)	2	1	4	3
(b)	1	2	4	3
(c)	2	4	1	3
(d)	2	1	3	4

11. Select the incorrect sentence.

(a) Blood has matrix containing proteins, salts and hormones
(b) Two bones are connected with ligament
(c) Tendons are non-fibrous tissue and elastic
(d) Cartilage is a form of connective tissue.

12. The velocity of sound is affected by change in

I. pressure II. wavelength
III. medium IV. temperature

Choose the correct option.
(a) I and II (b) III and IV
(c) I, II and IV (d) I, III and IV

13. The possible path(s) of cathode rays that are ejecting from cathode surface can be shown as

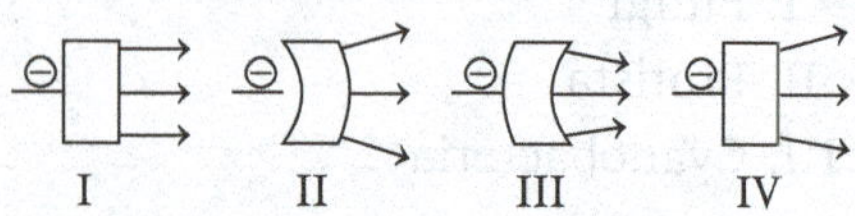

The correct images are
(a) I and II (b) I, II and III
(c) II, III and IV (d) Only I

14. Potential energy of a person is maximum when he is
(a) standing on roof
(b) sitting on the chair
(c) sitting on the ground
(d) lying down on ground

15. Match the property given in Column I with the example given in Column II and choose the correct answer using the codes given below the columns.

	Column I	Column II
A.	Randomly moving particles	1. Water
B.	Layers can slide over each other	2. Sugar
C.	Converts into solid under pressure	3. Nitrogen
D.	Particles are in fixed state	4. Carbon dioxide

Codes

	A	B	C	D
(a)	3	1	4	2
(b)	1	2	3	4
(c)	3	4	2	1
(d)	4	1	3	2

16. A key of a mechanical piano struck gently and then struck again but much harder this time in the second case.
(a) Sound will be louder but pitch will not be different
(b) Sound will be louder but pitch will also be higher
(c) Sound will be louder but pitch will be lower
(d) Both loudness and pitch will remain unaffected

17. Mitochondria have two membrane. The outer membrane is very .... *X* ...., while the inner membrane is .... *Y* ....
Choose the correct option for *X* and *Y* respectively.

	X	*Y*
(a)	Folded	Porous
(b)	Porous	Deeply folded
(c)	Rigid	Porous
(d)	Porous	Soft

18. The graph given below represents the uniform heating of a substance, starting from below its melting point, when the substance is in its solid state.

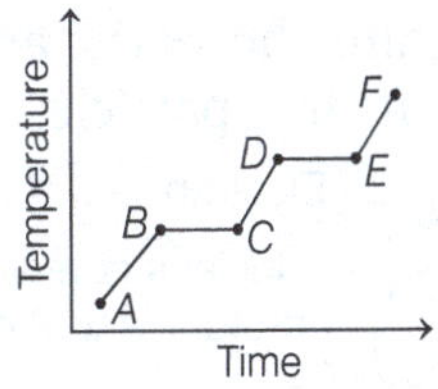

Which of the following line segments represents an increase in average kinetic energy?
(a) *AB* and *BC*
(b) *AB* and *CD*
(c) *BC* and *DE*
(d) *DE* and *EF*

19. Two identical bullets are fired, one by a light rifle and another by a heavy rifle with the same force. Which rifle will hurt the shoulder more?
(a) Lighter
(b) Heavier
(c) Both will hurt with same impact
(d) Neither will hurt at all

20. It there is low rainfall in a field area throughout the year, what measures you will not suggest to the farmers for better cropping.
(a) Reduced tilling
(b) Enrich soil with humus
(c) Use of drought resistant crops
(d) Use of late maturing crop varieties

21. A sprinter is running along the circumference of a big sports stadium with constant speed. Which of the following is not changing in this case?
I. Magnitude of acceleration being produced.

II. Distance covered by the sprinter per second.

III. Direction in which the sprinter is running.

IV. Centripetal force acting on the sprinter.

Codes

(a) I and II (b) III and IV

(c) I, II and IV (d) II, III and IV

22. The diagram shows the arrangement of electrons in a particle.

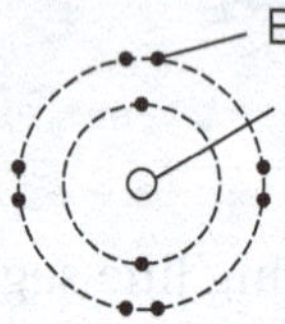

The symbol of the particle is

(a) N^{3-} (b) O^{2-} (c) F^{-} (d) Ne

23. Which of the following statements is correct?

I. Pitch of sound depends on its frequency.

II. Loudness of sound depends on its frequency.

III. Sound travels faster in air than in solids.

IV. Speed of sound in air varies with temperature.

Codes

(a) I and II (b) II and III

(c) I and IV (d) I, II and IV

24. Select the correct functional role of vacuole in a cell.

(a) Vacuoles do not help in maintaining rigidity of cell

(b) Vacuoles form thread-like tail in sperms of many mannals

(c) Vacuoles expell excess water and waste products form the cell

(d) Vacuoles store only excretory products of a cell

25. An airship is moving forwards at constant height.

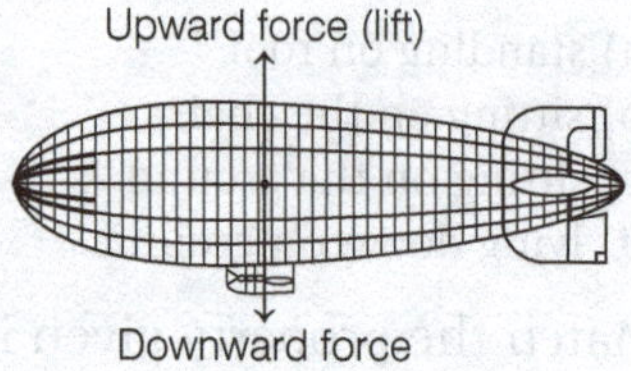

Which statement is correct?

(a) Gravity no longer has any effect

(b) The airship now has zero mass

(c) The potential energy is zero

(d) The upward and downward forces are balanced

26. The atomic mass of the lead is 208 and its atomic number is 82, the atomic mass of bismuth is 209 and its atomic number is 83. The ratio of the neutrons/protons

I. is higher in lead than bismuth.

II. is lower in bismuth than lead.

III. is equal in both lead and bismuth.

IV. does not depend on the above data.

The correct statement(s) is/are

(a) I and III (b) I and II

(c) Only IV (d) III and IV

27. Study the figure given below.

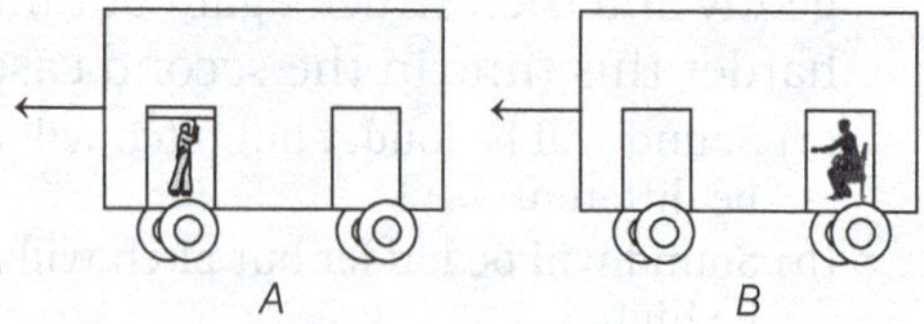

The man got hurt because

(a) due to inertia of rest, road is left behind and man reaches forward

(b) due to inertia of motion upper part of body continues to be in motion in forward direction while feet come to rest as soon as they touch the road

(c) he leans forward as a matter of habit

(d) of the combined effect of (a), (b) and (c)

28. Find out the correct sentence.

(a) Parenchyamatous tissues have not intercellular spaces.
(b) Collenchymatous tissues are irregularly thickened at corners.
(c) Apical and intercalary meristems are permanent tissues.
(d) All are correct statement

29. Which graph shows the temperature altering as steam at 110°C is cooled to –10°C?

(a)
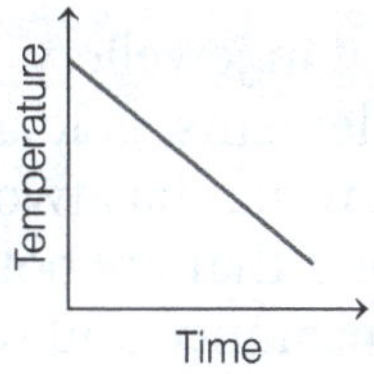

(b)
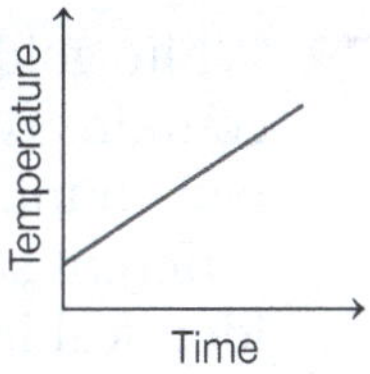

(c)
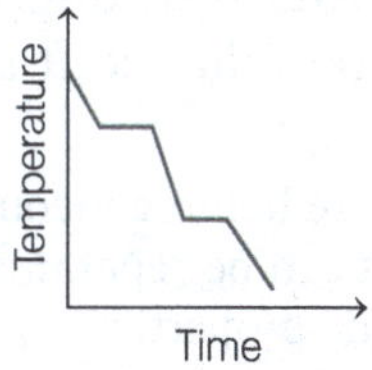

(d)
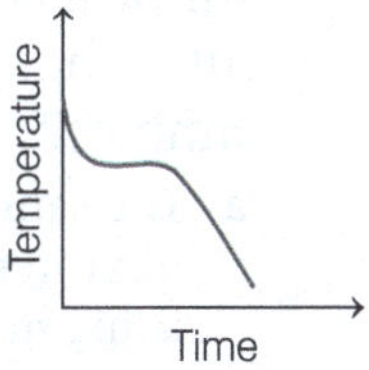

30. The specific gravity of a solid w.r.t. a liquid is $\frac{4}{5}$ and specific gravity of a liquid w.r.t. water is $\frac{10}{9}$, then the specific gravity of solid w.r.t. water is

(a) 18/25 (b) 8/9 (c) 0.56 (d) 1.8

31. Which of the following statements are true?

I. Cells have many different shapes and sizes.
II. All living things are made up of more than one cell.
III. The new cells formed from division are different from the parent cell.
IV. Cell walls are important to plants because they give the plant cells their shape.

Codes

(a) I and IV
(b) I, II and III
(c) II and IV
(d) I, II, III and IV

32. If velocity of an object decreases with time, then it is called

(a) retardation
(b) deceleration
(c) negative acceleration
(d) All of the above

33. Ashok took a compound X, one mole of which weigh 35 g. He made the following experimental set up.

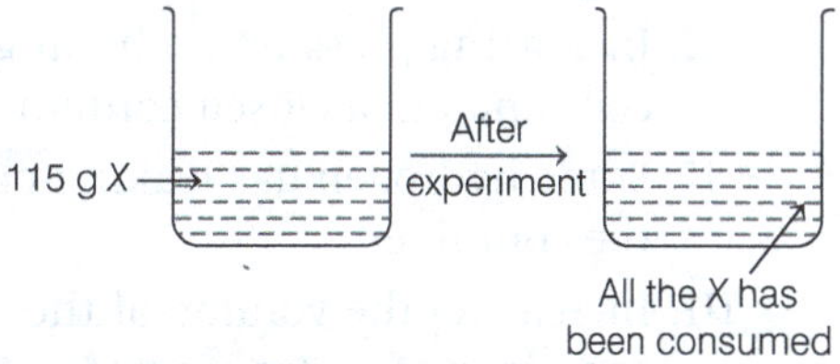

The compound X is

(a) ammonium hydroxide
(b) sodium hydroxide
(c) sodium chloride
(d) sodium peroxide

34. Identify the correct labels w.r.t A, B and C in the diagram given below. Name the part X, which transmits impulse away from the cell body.

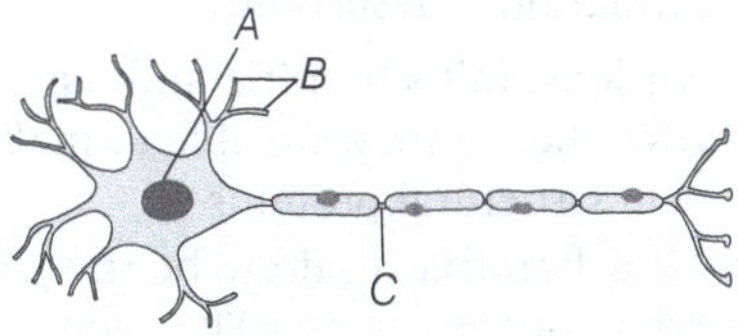

	A	*B*	*C*	*X*
(a)	Nucleus	Axon	Dendrites	Nucleus
(b)	Nucleus	Dendrites	Axon	Axon
(c)	Axon	Nucleus	Dendrites	Axon
(d)	Nucleus	Dendrites	Axon	Dendrites

35. A wave travels through a medium with a speed of 340 m/s. If the frequency of the wave is doubled, what happens to the wave speed and wavelength?

(a) Remains constant, doubles
(b) Doubles, reduced by a factor of two
(c) Remains constant, reduced by a factor of two
(d) Reduced by a factor of two, remains constant

36. In which of the following conditions, the distance between the molecules of hydrogen gas would increase?

I. Increasing pressure on hydrogen contained in a closed container.
II. Some hydrogen gas leaking out of the container.
III. Increasing the volume of the container of hydrogen gas.
IV. Adding more hydrogen gas to the container without increasing the volume of the container.

Choose the correct option.

(a) I and III (b) I and IV
(c) II and III (d) II and IV

37. Find out the false statement.

(a) Golgi apparatus is involved with the formation of lysosomes
(b) Nucleus, mitochondria and plastid have DNA, hence they are able to make their own structural proteins
(c) Mitochondria is said to be the power house of the cell as ATP is generated in them
(d) Cytoplasm is called as protoplasm

38. Anuj went to hill station with his family. He then did an experiment on a fact learnt in class. He clapped his hands near mountains and hears the echo after 8 s. If the speed of sound is $330\ ms^{-1}$, then the distance of the mountain from the Anuj was

(a) 2640 m
(b) 1320 m
(c) 660 m
(d) 2000 m

39. White gold used in jewellery contains two elements, gold and palladium. A jeweller has two different samples that are both identical in appearance and have a uniform composition through out. What can be said about the samples?

(a) The samples are heterogeneous mixtures that can be separated by using magnetic properties
(b) The samples have variable compositions and are classified as metallic solutions
(c) These are homogenous mixtures and can be classified as metallic alloys
(d) The materials are heterogenous mixtures and can be clasified by their components

40. Growing different crops on a piece of land in pre-planned succession is known as.......

(a) inter cropping
(b) mixed cropping
(c) organic farming
(d) crop rotation

2 Marks Questions

41. Rohit took a challenge to cover a distance of 1 km per minute on his bicycle. If he covers half the distance in 3/5th of a minute with what speed should he ride the remaining journey on his bicycle?

(a) 20 ms^{-1}

(b) 25 ms^{-1}

(c) 20.83 ms^{-1}

(d) 30 ms^{-1}

42. During an experiment hydorgen (H_2) and oxygen (O_2) gases reacted in an electric arc to produce water as follows

$$2H + O_2 \xrightarrow{\text{Electricity}} 2H_2O$$

The experiment is repeated three times and data tabulated as shown below.

Experiment number	Mass of H_2 reacted	Mass of O_2 reacted	Mass of H_2O produced
1	2g	16 g	18 g
2	4g	32 g	36 g
3	–		9 g

During 3rd experiment the researcher forgot to list masses of H_2 and O_2 used. So, if the law of constant proportion is correct then find mass of O_2 used during 3rd experiment.

(a) 4g (b) 8g

(c) 16g (d) 32g

43. An unripe green fruit changes colour when it ripens. The reason being

(a) chromoplast changes to chlorophyll

(b) chromoplasts changes to chromosomes

(c) chromosomes changes to chromoplast

(d) chloroplast changes to chromoplasts

44. A passenger tosses a coin in the moving train. A coin falls back as shown in the figure.

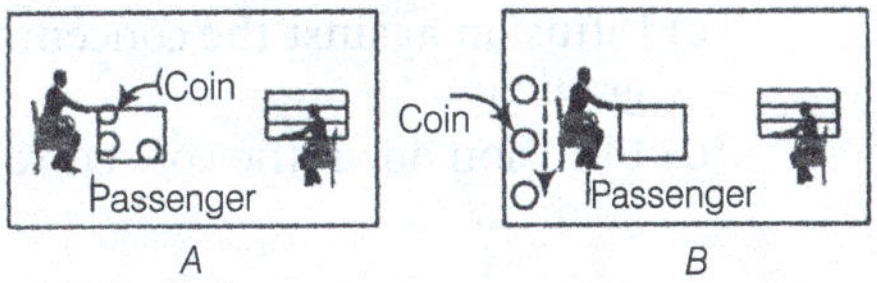

The above situation is possible if the motion of the train is

(a) accelerated

(b) non-uniform

(c) retarded

(d) along the circular track

45. Match the terms given in column I with their example given in column II and choose the correct answer using the codes given below the columns.

	Column I		Column II
A.	Solution	1.	Chalk in water
B.	Colloid	2.	Tincture of iodine
C.	Suspension	3.	Starch in water
D.	Homogeneous	4.	A mixture of chalk and sand
E.	Heterogeneous	5.	Air

Codes

	A	B	C	D	E
(a)	2	3	1	5	4
(b)	1	2	3	4	5
(c)	2	3	1	4	5
(d)	3	2	4	5	1

46. The arrows show the movement of salts into a cell.

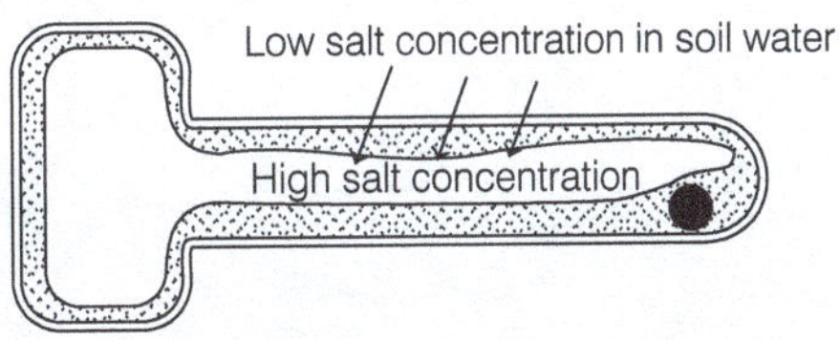

Which of the following correctly describes the movement?

(a) Active transport against the concentration gradient
(b) Active transport down the concentration gradient
(c) Diffusion against the concentration gradient
(d) Diffusion down the concentration gradient

47. Sonu whose mass is 5 kg. While playing, he runs up a flight of stairs 6.5 m high in 7 s. How much power does he develop?

(a) 0.019 W (b) 0.91 W
(c) 1.098 W (d) 45.5 W

48. Making antiviral drugs is more difficult than making anti-bacterial medicines because

(a) viruses make use of host machinery
(b) viruses are on the border line of living and non-living
(c) viruses have very few biochemical mechanisms of their own
(d) viruses have a protein coat

49. A car moves with a speed of 30 km/h for half an hour and 40 km/h for two hours, then the average speed of the car is

(a) 34.3 km/h (b) 35.3 km/h
(c) 33.3 km/h (d) 36.6 km/h

50. Column I represents the name of the compound and Column II represents the number of pieces will be required to form the compound. Match Column I with Column II and choose the correct option from the codes given below.

Column I	Column II
A. CO_2	1. 2
B. H_2O_2	2. 3
C. NO	3. 4
D. $C_6H_{12}O_6$	4. 24

Codes

	A	B	C	D		A	B	C	D
(a)	3	2	1	4	(b)	2	3	1	4
(c)	4	2	3	1	(d)	1	2	4	3

Hints & Solutions

Matter in Our Surroundings

1. (*b*) Dissolution of sugar into water suggests that each matter (here, sugar as well as water) is made up of tiny particles which have some spaces and particles of one substance (i.e. sugar) occupies the space present in between the particles of other substance (i.e. water).

2. (*a*) More the freedom of the particles to move around, i.e. weaker the intermolecular forces of attraction, higher is the kinetic energy of individual molecules.
Thus, the increasing order of KE is
III < IV < II < I.

3. (*a*) Alcohol molecules occupy the space present in between water molecules. So, the final volume is somewhat lesser than the sum of the volumes of the two solutions.

4. (*a*) Increasing the volume of container of hydrogen gas, distance between the molecules of hydrogen gas increases in container.

5. (*b*) Since, mass is constant (same), thus density depends only upon volume.
Since, the volume occupied by iron is smallest, so it is the densest metal.

6. (*c*) Forces of attraction are maximum in solids and least in gases. Liquids have intermediate forces of attraction.
Thus, the correct order of increasing forces of attraction is
oxygen < water < sugar

7. (*b*) At room temperature, substance *B* exists as a liquid which has the lower boiling point as compared to liquid *C*.

8. (*c*) From ideal gas equation,
$$pV = nRT$$
Thus, $$n = \frac{pV}{RT}$$
or $$\frac{n}{V} = \frac{p}{RT}$$
Thus, number of moles per litre $= \dfrac{p}{RT}$

9. (*b*) According to Charles' law,
$$V \propto T \text{ (at constant } p)$$
So, when temperature of water increases, it will result in increased volume due to expansion of gas at higher temperature.

10. (*a*) Because $pV = nRT$ or $pV = \dfrac{m}{M} RT$
$$pM = dRT$$
where, m is mass and M is molar mass.
Thus, $T \propto p$
$$\propto \frac{p}{d}$$
As temperature is directly proportional to the slope of p-d graph.
$\therefore \quad T_1 > T_2$

11. (*c*) Given, $V_1 = 600\text{ cm}^3$, $V_2 = ?$
$T_1 = 273 + 27°\text{C} = 300\text{ K}$
$T_2 = 273 + 7°\text{C} = 280\text{ K}$
According to Charles' law,
$$\frac{V_1}{T_1} = \frac{V_2}{T_2}$$
or $$V_2 = \frac{V_1 T_2}{T_1} = \frac{600 \times 280}{300} = 560\text{ cm}^3$$

12. (*b*) Gas molecules are always in continuous random motion, colliding with each other. Bromine being a heavier gas will diffuse slower than oxygen gas.

13. (*c*) The rate of evaporation is highest in beaker *C* having greater surface area because moving fan removes the moist air present above the liquid state immediately and the surface area of beaker *C* is greater than beaker *B*.

14. (*a*) Just as a solid is directly converted into gas, its reverse is also true. Although, this process is not shown in the given diagram. This process is called de-sublimation or deposition.

15. (*b*) Whenever a liquid solidifies, i.e. convert into its solid state, energy is released. This is because liquid has energy of fusion but solid does not, which it emits when converted into solid state.

16. (*d*) When a gas is heated, the speed of gas molecules and the average number of gas molecules hitting the wall per second increases due to which kinetic energy also increases. But the average distance between the gas molecules remains the same.

17. (*c*) Lower the mass, more is the rate of diffusion. Only mass of methane (CH_4, 16 u) is lower than that of oxygen (O_2, 32u), so in case of methane, the water level at *Y* rises.

18. (*b*) The temperature remains constant during the melting process as the heat is utilised for the conversion of solid into liquid as latent heat of fusion.

19. (*c*) Temperature, $T = 180°F$

$$\frac{°C - 0}{100} = \frac{°F - 32}{180}$$

$$\frac{°C}{100} = \frac{180 - 32}{180}$$

$$°C = \frac{148 \times 100}{180} = 82$$

Further, $K = 273 + t°C = 273 + 82 = 355\,K$

20. (*b*) Given, $n = 5.52 \times 10^{-2}$mol

$V = 413\,mL = 413 \times 10^{-3}\,L$

$T = 88°C = 88 + 273\,K = 361\,K,$

$R = 0.0821\,L\text{-atm/mol}^{-1}K^{-1}$

From ideal gas law, $pV = nRT$

$$p = \frac{nRT}{V}$$

$$= \frac{5.52 \times 10^{-2} \times 0.0821 \times 361}{413 \times 10^{-3}}$$

$$= 3.96 \approx 4$$

21. (*b*) The gas which obeys gas laws under all the conditions of temperature and pressure is called ideal gas.
As the volume of a specific amount of gas, at 27°C decreases, its pressure increases.
According to the Boyle's law, $p \propto \frac{1}{V}$
At constant temperature, volume of a gas is inversely proportional to pressure.

22. (*b*) **Boyle's law** At constant temperature,

$$p \propto \frac{1}{V}$$

Charles' law At constant pressure,

$$V \propto T$$

Avogadros' law At constant pressure and temperature,

$$V \propto n$$

Ideal gas equation At constant *n* and *T*,

$$V \propto \frac{1}{p}$$

At constant *n* and *p*

$$V \propto T$$

23. (*a*) (I), (II) and (III) represent Boyle's law which is $p \propto \frac{1}{V}$ or pV is constant at constant temperature.

Is Matter Around Us Pure?

1. (*c*) Presence of three electrons in the valence shell suggests that the element belong to group 13 and has valency 3. Only three shells filled with electrons suggest that it is present in third period, so it must be aluminium and the nature of aluminium oxide is amphoteric.

2. (*c*) Diatomic means element containing two atoms. Formulae/symbols of given elements are H_2 (hydrogen), F_2 (fluorine), Ne(neon), N_2 (nitrogen), Cl_2 (chlorine), O_2(oxygen).

3. (*a*) Product *Z* is formed by the combination of *X* and *Y*, thus has more mass than that of *X* and *Y* separately. Also *Z* is entirely a new product, thus cannot show same properties, as of *X* and *Y*.

4. (*b*) Concentration in terms of mass by mass per cent of solvent

$$= \frac{320}{40 + 320} \times 100 = 88.9\% \approx 89\%$$

5. (*a*) Mass of solute = 50 g
Mass of solvent = 450 g
Mass of solution = Mass of solute + Mass of solvent

$$= 450 + 50 = 500\,g$$

Mass percentage of solution

$$= \frac{\text{Mass of solute}}{\text{Mass of solution}} \times 100$$

$$= \frac{50}{500} \times 100 = 10\%$$

6. (*b*) The amount added by Ravi is 90 g or 0.09 kg. Since, the amount required to prepare a saturated solution is 0.1 kg which is greater than the amount available.
So, he get only an unsaturated solution.

7. (*a*) Tyndall effect is due to the scattering and polarising of light by small suspended particles.

8. (*b*) In I, III, IV scattering of a beam of light occur by a medium containing small suspended particles. But when normal light passes through copper sulphate solution due to its small particle size, they do not scatter a beam of light passing through the solution.

9. (*b*) Burning of a candle is physical as well as chemical change. On heating, candle wax gets melted, since it again turns into solid wax on cooling. So, the melting of wax and vaporisation of melted wax are physical change. The process of burning is a chemical reaction, so it is a chemical change.
Sublimation of ammonium chloride is the process of change of state from solid directly into vapour. So, it is a physical change. Ammonium chloride decomposes into ammonia and hydrochloric acid, so it is a chemical change also.
Crystallisation of copper sulphate is a physical change.

10. (*b*) Chemical composition of oil and water are different that's why, they differ in their odour as well as in inflammability.

11. (*a*) Germanium, arsenic and antimony possess some properties of metals and some properties of non-metals. So, they are classified as metalloids. H_2, O_2 and N_2 are elements because elements contain only one type of atom. All homogeneous mixtures are not pure, i.e. true solution. Mercury and bromine are the only two liquids elements in which mercury is a metal whether bromine is a non-metal.

12. (*a*) Alcohol and water both are liquids, so their solution is an example of liquid in liquid type solution.
Amalgamated zinc contains mercury and zinc metal. Mercury exists in liquid state so, it is a liquid in solid type solution.
Aqueous solution of sodium chloride is an example of solid in liquid type solution.
Aerated water is the water in which a gas is dissolved in water. So, it is an example of gas in liquid type solution.

13. (*a*) Supersaturated solutions contain more amount of solute that a solvent can hold at a given temperature. These solutions are stable only at high temperature.

14. (*d*) Rusting of iron is a chemical change because the composition of rust is different from that of the iron. Similarly, baking of cake is also a chemical change, melting of wax is a physical change while burning of wick and gases is a chemical change.

15. (*c*) A chemical change happens when the molecular identity of matter changes to an entirely new form. Temperature change is one major indicator of a chemical change.
Colour changes when two solution react and when a chemical reaction produces a gaseous product, this is an indication that a chemical change is occurring.

16. (*d*) In chemical reactions, some changes are found in products and reactants. So, chemical change has also effect on physical properties.
Drying of paint is both physical as well as chemical change.
Physical change because the state of paint changes on drying and chemical because the paint combines with gases in the atmosphere.
Evaporation is a physical change in which water changes into gaseous state from liquid state. Decantation is a chemical change.

17. (*c*)

S. No.	Example	Type	Dispersed Phase	Dispersed Medium
I.	Rubber	Foam	Gas	Solid
II.	Face cream	Emulsion	Liquid	Liquid
III.	Coloured gemstone	Solid sol	Solid	Solid
IV.	Butter	Gel	Liquid	Solid
V.	Cloud	Aerosol	Liquid	Gas

18. (*d*) Since, *X* and *Y* cannot be broken down into simpler substances by simple chemical reactions, so these must be elements. *P* is formed, when *X* and *Y* combine together. So, it must be a compound and composition of a compound is always fixed.

19. (*c*) Metal is a substance consists of only a single type of constituent particles.
In heterogeneous mixture, visible boundaries of separation between its consituents can be seen early.
In compounds constituents lose their properties. Chemical reaction does not take place during formation of mixture.

20. (*c*) Solution of copper sulphate does not exhibit Tyndall effect.
Sugar solution is a homogeneous solution, because any substance dissolve in water is homogeneous mixture.
Solubility of gases decreases with increase in temperature.

Atoms and Molecules

1. (a) The valency of M is 3.
Charge on phosphate ion is – 3.

$$\underset{+3}{M}\underset{-3}{PO_4} \equiv MPO_4$$

2. (c) Since, nitrogen exhibits variable valency, so its equivalent mass is also variable. That's why, law of definite proportions is not applicable to its oxides.

3. (c) 112 mL volume is occupied by 0.220 g
∴ 22400 mL volume is occupied by

$$= \frac{0.220 \times 22400}{112}$$

$= 44$ g (molecular mass of the gas)

(a) $NO_2 = 14 + 32 = 46$ u
(b) $NO = 14 + 16 = 30$ u
(c) $CO_2 = 12 + 32 = 44$ u
(d) $C_3H_6 = 36 + 6 = 42$ u

Hence, the gas is CO_2.

4. (c) The valency of P is 2.
Charge on fluoride ion is –1

$$\underset{2}{P}\ \underset{-1}{F} \equiv PF_2$$

5. (d) In carbon disulphide, the mass ratio is

$$\frac{C}{S} = \frac{12}{64} = \frac{3}{16}$$

Thus, 3 g of carbon combines with 16 g of sulphur.

6. (c) Mass given-Barium chloride = 107.2 g
Sodium sulphate = 116.1 g
Mass of beaker = 150 g
Total = 107.2 + 116.1 + 150 = 373.3 g
The student C has mass of reaction mixture in the beaker 373.3 g. Hence, this observation obeys the law of conservation of mass.

7. (b) Percentage of carbon in sample A.

$$= \frac{1.2}{1.2 + 3.2} \times 100 = 27.3\%$$

Percentage of oxygen in sample A.

$$= \frac{3.2}{1.2 + 3.2} \times 100 = 72.7\%$$

Since, in the given two samples, the composition of constituents is fixed, so the data are in accordance with law of definite proportions.

8. (b) $\underset{6.3\text{ g}}{NaHCO_3} + \underset{15\text{ g}}{CH_3COOH} \longrightarrow \underset{18\text{ g}}{\text{Residue}} + \underset{x\text{g}}{CO_2}$

According to law of conservation of mass,
Mass of reactants = Mass of products

$$6.3 + 15 = 18 + x$$

$$\Rightarrow x = 6.3 + 15 - 18 = 3.3 \text{ g}$$

9. (b) Mass of 94.91 mL nitrogen at STP

$$= \frac{28 \times 94.91}{22400} = 0.1186 \text{ g}$$

Amount of hydrogen present $= \frac{0.1186}{0.5} \times 100$
$= 23.72\%$

Amount of oxygen present
$= [100 - (40.67 + 8.47 + 23.72)]\ \% = 27.14\%$

∴ Ratio of number of atoms of C, H, N, O are the compound.

$$C : H : N : O = \frac{40.67}{12} : \frac{8.47}{1} : \frac{23.72}{14} : \frac{27.14}{16}$$

$$= 3.39 : 8.47 : 1.69 : 1.7$$

$$= 2 : 5 : 1 : 1$$

Empirical formula of compound is C_2H_5NO.

10. (b) A. Water, H_2O

$$\text{Ratio of H/O} = \frac{2 \times 1}{16} = \frac{1}{8} = 1 : 8$$

B. Ammonia, NH_3

$$\text{Ratio of N/H} = \frac{14}{1 \times 3} = 14 : 3$$

C. Carbon dioxide, CO_2

$$\text{Ratio of C/O} = \frac{12}{2 \times 16} = \frac{12}{32} = 3 : 8$$

D. Sulphur dioxide, SO_2

$$\text{Ratio of S/O} = \frac{32}{2 \times 16} = \frac{32}{32} = 1 : 1$$

11. (a) $\underset{20.8\text{ g}}{BaCl_2} + \underset{9.8\text{ g}}{H_2SO_4} \longrightarrow \underset{7.3\text{ g}}{HCl} + \underset{x\text{ g}}{BaSO_4}$

According to law of conservation of mass,
mass of reactants = mass of products

$$20.8 + 9.8 = 7.3 + x$$

$$\Rightarrow x = 23.3 \text{ g}$$

12. (b) The following are the balanced equations

$$4Fe(s) + 3O_2(g) \longrightarrow 2Fe_2O_3(s)$$

$$2Mg(s) + O_2(g) \longrightarrow 2MgO(s)$$

$$CH_4(g) + 2O_2(g) \longrightarrow CO_2(g) + 2H_2O(g)$$

The unbalanced equation is

$$P_4(s) + O_2(g) \longrightarrow P_4O_{10}(s)$$

It can be balanced as follows:

$$P_4(s) + 5O_2(g) \longrightarrow P_4O_{10}(s)$$

According to the law of conservation of mass
Total mass of reactants = Total mass of products

13. (a) On fixing the mass of dinitrogen as 28 g, the masses of combining dioxygen are 32, 64, 32 and

80 in the given four oxides. These are in the simple whole number ratio, i.e. 2 : 4 : 2 : 5. Hence, the given data obey the law of multiple proportions.

14. (*c*) The symbol of silver is Ag. Noble gases are monoatomic. Molecular mass of ethyne is 26 g/mol.

15. (*b*) $K_2CO_3 = 2 \times 39 + 12 + 3 \times 16 = 138\ u$

$Na_2O = 2 \times 23 + 16$
$= 46 + 16 = 62\ u$

$HNO_3 = 1 + 14 + 3 \times 16 = 63\ u$

$SO_2 = 32 + 2 \times 16 = 64\ u$

16. (*d*) Al (charge + 3) and (SO_4) (charge − 2), crossed: $= Al_2(SO_4)_3$

17. (*d*)

Ion	Formula	Atomicity
I.Ammonium	NH_4^+	5
II.Nitrate	NO_3^-	4
III.Hydrogen carbonate	HCO_3^-	5
IV.Sulphate	SO_4^{2-}	5
V.Phosphate	PO_4^{3-}	5
VI.Sulphite	SO_3^{2-}	4

Except II and VI, all are penta-atomic ions.

18. (*b*) A. Calcium oxide, CaO

$40 + 16 = 56\ u$

B. Magnesium chloride, $MgCl_2$

$24 + 2 \times 35.5 = 95\ u$

C. Aluminium phosphide, AlP

$27 + 31 = 58\ u$

D. Calcium carbonate, $CaCO_3$

$40 + 12 + 3 \times 16$
$= 40 + 12 + 48 = 100\ u$

19. (*a*) Hydrochloric acid is secreted from the stomach and helps in carbohydrate metabolism. When an excess amount of HCl is present in the stomach and less carbohydrate is taken as food, acidity occurs. The mass of salt and water formed is equal to the combined mass of $Mg(OH)_2$ and HCl.

20. (*c*) $AlCl_3 = 27 \times 1 + 35.5 \times 3 = 133.5\ u$

$CaCO_3 = 40 \times 1 + 12 \times 1 + 16 \times 3 = 100\ u$

$Cu\ (NO_3)_2 = 63.5 \times 1 + 62 \times 2 = 187.5\ u$

$NaHCO_3 = 23 \times 1 + 1 + 12 + 16 \times 3 = 84\ u$

21. (*b*) The molecular formula of ferrous sulphate is $FeSO_4$, because valency of ferrous ion is Fe^{+2} and sulphate ion SO_4^{2-}.
The molecular formula of ferric sulphate is $Fe_2(SO_4)_3$ because, valency of ferric ion is Fe^{+3}.

22. (*b*) Weight of zinc required = 22.65% of total weight

$$= \frac{22.65}{100} \times 20 = 4.53\ g$$

23. (*d*) $\underset{10\ g}{CaCO_3} \xrightarrow{\Delta} \underset{5.6\ g}{CaO} + \underset{4.4\ g}{CO_2}$

According to law of conservation of mass.
Mass of reactants = Mass of products.
Atomic mass shows how many times an atom of that element is heavier than 1/12th of the mass of C-12 atom.
In CO and CO_2, the masses of oxygen combining with the same mass of carbon are in the simple whole number ratio (i.e. 1 : 2). This is in accordance with law of multiple proportions.
The statement given in reason obeys law of reciprocal proportions. 1u = 1/12th of mass of C-12 because C-12 isotope was selected as standard.

24. (*b*) In compound *A*,
1.00 g nitrogen combines with oxygen = 0.57 g
In compound *B*,
2.00 g nitrogen combines with oxygen = 2.24 g
∴ 1.00 g nitrogen will combine with oxygen

$$= \frac{2.24}{2} = 1.12\ g$$

In compound *C*,
3.00 g nitrogen combines with oxygen = 5.11 g
∴ 1.00 g nitrogen will combine with oxygen

$$= \frac{5.11}{3} = 1.70\ g$$

Thus, the ratio of masses of oxygen combining with 1 g of nitrogen is 0.57 : 1.12 : 1.70 = 1 : 2 : 3, i.e. it is in whole number ratio.
Thus, the results obey law of multiple proportions.

25. (*c*) Mass = moles × molecular mass

(a) 0.2 mole of sucrose (∵ molecular mass of sucrose = 342 u)
Mass = 0.2 × 342 = 68.4 g

(b) 2 moles of CO_2 (∵ molecular mass of CO_2 = 12 + 32 = 44 u)
Mass = 2 × 44 = 88 g

(c) 2 moles of $CaCO_3$ ($\because$ molecular mass of $CaCO_3$ = 100 u)

Mass = $2 \times 100 = 200$ g

(d) 10 moles of H_2O ($\because$ molecular mass of H_2O = 18 u)

Mass = $10 \times 18 = 180$ g

Thus, weight of 2 moles of $CaCO_3$ (*z*) is the highest.

26. (*b*) The correct matching is

Ion	Formula
Carbonate	CO_3^{2-}
Hydroxide	OH^-
Sulphate	SO_4^{2-}
Phosphate	PO_4^{3-}

27. (*c*) The correct matching is

Ion	Formula
Sulphite	SO_3^{2-}
Sulphide	S^{2-}
Sulphate	SO_4^{2-}
Bisulphite	HSO_3^-

28. (*a*) The correct matching is

Compound	Chemical formulae
Carbon monoxide	CO
Hydrogen chloride	HCl
Aluminium fluoride	AlF_3
Magnesium sulphide	MgS

Structure of the Atom

1. (*b*) The given particle is negatively charged. Proton carries a charge of one unit (positive) and mass of 1.6×10^{-27} g which is equal to 1 amu.

2. (*d*) This is the Rutherford model because neutrons were not discovered up to that time. Rutherford used α-particles, composition of which is $({}_2^4He)^{2+}$, i.e. helium nuclei.

3. (*d*) It is not proposed by Bohr.
Note The given statement is infact uncertainty principle, about which you will read in higher classes.

4. (*b*) Opposite charges are developed on rubbing the hair with balloon because these charges attract each other.

5. (*b*) In order to explain the stability of an atom, Niels Bohr gave a new arrangement of electrons in the atom that was based on the concept that the electrons do not radiate energy while revolving in fixed orbits.

6. (*a*) Mass number = Number of p^+ + Number of n^0

$= 4 + 5 = 9$

Thus, the symbol is ${}_4^9Be$.

Since, the atom is electrically neutral, so number of electrons = number of protons = 4

7. (*c*) According to Bohr's model, *K* or 1st shell can accommodate a maximum of 2 electrons and *L* or 2nd shell can accommodate a maximum of 8 electrons.
Thus, II and IV are not in accordance with Bohr's rule.

8. (*b*) Mass number = Number of protons + Number of neutrons

$\therefore$ Number of protons

= Mass number − number of neutrons

$= 27 - 14 = 13$

In case of positive ion,
Number of electrons

= Number of protons − Total positive charge

$= 13 - 3 = 10$

Thus, the ion contains 10 electrons.

9. (*d*) The electronic configuration of Mg (12) atom is 2, 8, 2. In the formation of Mg^{2+} ion, two electrons are lost from outermost shell, hence the configuration becomes 2, 8.
Thus, the electronic structure of Mg^{2+} ion is

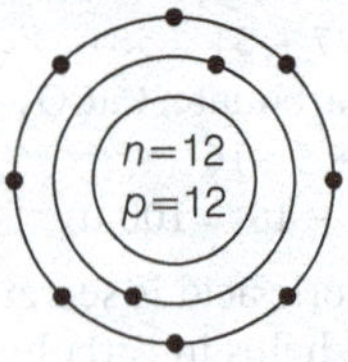

Note Number of neutrons and protons remain unaffected during the formation of ion.

10. (*d*) ${}_{17}^{35}Cl$, Number of $p^+ = 17$

Number of $n^0 = 35 - 17 = 18$

${}_{17}^{37}Cl$, Number of $p^+ = 17$

Number of $n^0 = 37 - 17 = 20$

11. (*a*) Cl exists mainly as ${}^{35}Cl$ and ${}^{37}Cl$ isotopes (with different number of neutrons).

The relative atomic mass would be the weighted average of the relative isotopic masses of the isotopes.

12. (*a*) Mass of electron $= 9.1 \times 10^{-31}$ kg

Mass of proton $= 1.67 \times 10^{-27}$ kg

Mass of neutron $= 1.675 \times 10^{-27}$ kg

Mass of α-particle $= 6.67 \times 10^{-27}$ kg

So, increasing order of *e/m* for *e, p, n* and α-particle is $n < \alpha < p < e$.

($\because$ neutron has no charge)

13. (*a*)

Subatomic particle	Discoverer
A. Proton	Goldstein
B. Electron	Thomson
C. Neutron	Chadwick
D. Positron	Anderson

14. (*a*) An ion has less or more number of electrons than protons. If ion has more number of electrons than protons then it will be an anion. If ion has less number of electrons than protons then it will be a cation.

15. (*d*) Comparing the given value of *e/m* shows that the charge on the particle of the cathode rays is 2000 times larger than that on the H^+ ion and the cathode ray particle is 2000 times smaller in mass than the H-atom.

16. (*c*) The chronological order of different atomic models is

I. Thomson's atomic model

II. Rutherford's atomic model

III. Bohr's atomic model

17. (*b*) Thomson's model suggested the uniform distribution of mass all over the atom.

According to this model, an atom contains a sphere of positive charge, in which negatively charged electrons are studded uniformly.

The positive charge (due to protons) and negative charge (due to electrons) balance each other.

18. (*a*) Dalton told us about atom, that atom is smallest particle of any substance and it is not divisible.

Neils Bohr told about stationary orbits.

Goldstein was the discoverer of canal rays.

Rutherford explain about nucleus in their α-particle experiment.

19. (*a*) Deflection of α-particles away from the nucleus suggested that nucleus is the positively charged. This model can be compared to solar system, so also known by the name planetary model.

20. (*c*) $Y = 2, 8, 6$

Since, it has 2 electrons less than octet, so its ion carry 2 – charge.

Only electrons are present in the shells, protons are always present in the nucleus. Being negatively charged, it is a non-metal and hence, form ionic compound with metals like sodium.

21. (*b*) When the atomic number is 6, electronic configuration is *K*-2, *L*-4, *M*-0, *N*-0.

When atomic number is 20, configuration is *K*-2, *L*-8, *M*-8, *N*-2.

So, $X = 2, Y = 4$ and $Z = 2$

22. (*d*) I. Cl^- $(17 + 1 = 18)$

Br^- $(35 + 1 = 36)$

I^- $(53 + 1 = 54)$

II. F^- $(9 + 1 = 10)$

Ne (10)

Na^+ $(11 - 1 = 10)$

III. K^+ $(19 - 1 = 18)$,

Ca^{2+} $(20 - 2 = 18)$,

Br^- $(35 + 1 = 36)$

IV. Li^+ $(3 - 1 = 2)$,

Na^+ $(11 - 1 = 10)$,

K^+ $(19 - 1 = 18)$

23. (*c*) Isotopes are the species having same atomic number but different mass number.

Because of the same atomic number, their electronic configuration and hence, the chemical properties are same.

However, they possess different physical properties.

24. (*c*) Isotones have same number of neutrons.

${}_6C^{14}$ $(14 - 6 = 8)$, ${}_7N^{15}$ $(15 - 7 = 8)$,

${}_9F^{17}$ $(17 - 9 = 8)$, ${}_6C^{12} = (12 - 6 = 6)$,

${}^{14}_{7}N$ $(14 - 7 = 7)$, ${}^{19}_{9}F$ $(19 - 9 = 10)$

25. (*a*) A. ${}^{16}_{8}O$, ${}^{17}_{8}O$, ${}^{18}_{8}O$ are isotopes.

B. ${}^{40}_{18}Ar$, ${}^{40}_{19}K$, ${}^{40}_{20}Ca$ are isobars.

C. ${}^{14}_{6}C$, ${}^{15}_{7}N$, ${}^{16}_{8}O$ are isotones.

(each has 8 neutrons).

D. O^{2-}, Na^+, Mg^{2+} are isoelectronics (each contains 10 electrons)

26. (*c*) J.J. Thomson's plum pudding model of atom had negatively charged electrons embedded within a positively charged soup. Rutherford concluded from the α-particles scattering experiment that positive charge of an atom occupies in nucleus of an atom.
We move away from the nucleus, the energy of orbits increases.

27. (*d*) Innermost atomic shell can hold a maximum of 2 electrons. The number of protons in Na^+ is 11. There is no effect of charge on number of protons.
Element having electronic configuration 2,7. It gains an electron from metal and complete it's octet. Elements with valency 1 are metals as well as halogen compounds.

28. (*b*) Average atomic mass $= \dfrac{A_1R_1 + A_2R_2}{R_1 + R_2}$

(Here, R_1 and R_2 = relative abundance, A_1 and A_2 = mass number)

$\therefore$ Available atomic mass

$$= \frac{79 \times 0.497 + 81 \times 0.503}{0.497 + 0.503} = 80.066 \approx 80$$

29. (*a*) Tincture of iodine = 5.7% of Iodine +H_2O + alcohol antiseptic. Isobars have different atomic number but same mass number. Their chemical property is different because there is a difference in number of e^-. Sodium-24 is used to detect blood clots. Cobalt-60 is used in the inspection of materials to reveal internal structure. Isobars have different electronic configuration.

30. (*a*)

Particle	Charge	Mass (u)	Deflection
p	1+	1	Attracted to negative plate
n	0	1	No deflection
e^-	1–	Negligible	Attracted to positive plate, greater deflection as it is much lighter

31. (*d*) Number of protons (and electrons) or atomic number are same in case of isotopes.
Let, number of proton = Y
Number of n^0 in $^{238}X = 238 - Y$
Number of n^0 in $^{235}X = 235 - Y$
Thus, ^{238}X has 3 more neutrons but no more electrons.

32. (*c*) Number of neutrons, $n^0 = 235 - 92 = 143$

Number of $p^+ = 92$

$$\text{Ratio of } \frac{n}{p} = \frac{143}{92} = 1.55$$

The Fundamental Unit of Life

1. (*c*) Organism *A* is a multicellular organism as it can be seen with naked eyes. It is a plant which is regarded as multicellular organism.

2. (*c*) *X* is a bacterial cell, which is prokaryotic in nature.
Y is an amoeboid cell and *Z* is a sperm of mammal. Both *Y* and *Z* are eukaryotic cells.

3. (*c*) A- In the year 1665. Robert Hooke discovered the cell.
B-The cell theory was given by two German biologists, a botanist MJ Schleieden in 1838 and zoologist T Schwann in 1839.
C-Robert Brown discovered the nucleus in 1831.
D-In 1839 Purkinje coined the term protoplasm.

4. (*b*) *A*—Cell wall, *B*—Cell membrane
C—Protoplasm, *D*—Vacuole
Cell membrane is a selectively permeable membrane, which control entry and exist of substances in the cell. Therefore, uptake of nitrate ions are control by cell membrane.

5. (*a*) *A*—Long hollow tubes formed by xylem, and their cell membrane joined end to end without any cross wall. They have no protoplasm.
Hence, contain no cytoplasm.
B—RBCs have cytoplasm.
C—Root hair cells also have cytoplasm.
D—Muscle cell also have cytoplasm.

6. (*d*) The correct option is 'd' as
A- Cytoplasm *C*-Chloroplast
B-Nucleus *D*-Intercellular space

7. (*c*) Lysosome secretes hydrolytic enzymes, which digest all content of cell and it will eventually die.

8. (*d*) The cell theory (shown in diagram) expanded by Virchow suggest that all cells arise from pre-existing cells.

9. (*a*) Nitrate ions enter into root hair cells by active transport, oxygen by diffusion and water by osmosis.

10. (*d*) Wilting is the loss of rigidity in the non-woody regions of plants.
It reduces the plant's ability to transpire and grow. Permanent wilting leads to plant death.

11. (*a*) In beaker *A*, raisins are placed in water which act as hypotonic solution as a result of endosmosis take place which involve movement of water inside the raisins, whereas in beaker *B*, raisins are placed in concentrated sugar solution which act as a hypertonic solution as a result exosmosis take place and raisins shrink.

12. (*d*) The correct option is 'd' as
It depicts the phenomenon of osmosis which involves the movement of water molecules (*Y*) through semi-permeable membrane from the region of its higher concentration to its lower concentration region ($A \rightarrow B$)

13. (*b*) The cell wall and chloroplast are the important structures of a plant cell, which are absent in the animal cell.
As the cell membrane is the outermost structure in animal cell while the plant cell have cell wall as the outermost covering. Whereas, the cytoplasm is present in both animal and plant cell.

14. (*c*) As RBC is placed in a strong salt solution, which is hypertonic in nature, therefore water moves out of the cell through osmosis and the cell will shrinks.

15. (*d*) The correct option is 'd' as rest all the options are related to the above paragraph mentioned in question while, option 'd' is the odd one out.

16. (*a*) Spongy mesophyll → Cell
Organ → Leaf, heart and kidney
Tissue → Root hair and xylem
Organ system → Skeleton
Organism → Worm.

17. (*b*) *P*—Cell wall, *Q*—Chloroplast. As cell wall and chloroplast are present only in plant cell.
R—Cell membrane, which is found in both animal and plant cells.
S—Centriole, which are present only in animal cells.

18. (*c*) *A*—Endoplasmic reticulum, *B*—Golgi body
C—Chloroplast
Out of three, chloroplast contains both DNA and ribosomes.

19. (*d*) The correct option is 'd' as all the given statements are incorrect and can be corrected as

I. Cell wall of prokaryotic cell is made up of peptidoglycan.
II. Spindle fibres are absent in prokaryotic cells while they are present in eukaryotic cells.
III. Prokaryotic cell have 70S ribosome.
IV. Flagella have 9 + 2 arrangement.

20. (*b*) Both A and R are true, but R is not the correct explanation of A.
Plasma membrane is called selectively permeable membrane as it permit the entry and exit of selective materials in and out of the cell.

21. (*c*) During day, light reaction take place in granum of chloroplast, whereas during night, dark reaction take place in stroma of the chloroplast. Both these processes lead to synthesis of food by the process of photosynthesis.

22. (*c*) Acrosome is the upper part or tip of an animal sperm, which is made up with the help of Golgi complex.

23. (*a*) Statements I and IV are not true and can be corrected as

I. Endoplasmic reticulum and Golgi body are involve in the formation of lysosomes.
IV. Cytoplasm is all the content inside the cell membrane excluding the nucleus. Whereas, protoplasm include cytoplasm and nucleus of the cell.

24. (*b*) Erythrocytes which are also known as RBCs lacks nucleus and most cell organelles including ER and mitochondria. Prokaryotic cells also lacks membrane bound cell organelles.

25. (*c*) (i) Potato–Leucoplast as these are colourless organelles in which material such as starch, oils and protein are stored.
(ii) Tomato–Chromoplast as these are coloured plastids contain various red pigments.
(iii) Spinach–Chloroplast as it contains green coloured pigment called chlorophyll.

26. (*a*) The correct answer is option 'a' as
The ovum is responsible for continuity of life because it will develop and form new individual.
Option (b) represents fat cells that store fat. Option 'c' represents bone cell is present in the bones and option 'd' represents muscle cell, which is present in the muscles.

27. (*c*) The correct option is option 'c' as
Plain water acts as hypotonic medium for raisins.
The dried raisins are placed in plain water, raisins swell up due to osmotic entry of water into raisins. Thus, endosmosis occurs.
While when swollen raisins transferred to a concentrated solution then raisins shrink. Concentrated solution is hypertonic medium for swollen raisins. Thus, exosomosis occur.

28. (*c*) Root hair becomes turgid due to osmosis. Hair cell aids supports. It is itself supported by the sap it contains. Xylem vessel is lignified and contains no cytoplasm or cell membrane when mature enough, cannot take up water by osmosis. It can provide support to plant, but not due to turgor pressure.

29. (*b*) Phagocytosis is a type of endocytosis in which cell ingest or engulf other cell or particle of food. It is also known as cell-eating.

30. (*b*) The correct option is 'b' as
The cytoplasm is general mass of protoplasm excluding nucleus, which contains the organelles, vitamins, enzymes and sugar. The nucleoplasm consists of the nucleolus and chromosome. Rest statement III is incorrect.

31. (*b*) The diagram shows a typical plant cell distinguished from animal cells by the presence of a cell wall, chloroplasts and a large central vacuole.
Statement III is not useful because it is important to state the size and location of the vacuole rather than just the fact that there is one vacuole.
Statement IV is also not useful because both animal and plant cells have mitochondria to release energy through the process of respiration.

32. (*c*) The correct option is 'c' as
Both chloroplast and mitochondria are not considered as the part of endomembrane system because they do not have coordinated functions.
Both are double membrane bound organelles containing 70S ribosome.

33. (*d*) Statement I is not conclusive enough as Many animal cells do not have visible vacuoles. There is presence of a large central vacuole in the diagram indicates that this is a plant cell. Statement II is correct since the large central vacuole in mature plant cells typically pushes the cytoplasm to the sides of the cell.
Statements III and IV are correct since, plant cells contain both chloroplasts and a cell, wall both of which are absent in animal cells.

34. (*c*) Golgi body (*X*) is involved in the formation of lysosomes. It has a system of membrane bound vesicles arranged parallel to each other in stack called cisternae.
Lysosomes (*Y*) are also called as suicidal bags as it contains digestive enzymes made by Rough Endoplasmic Reticulum or RER (*Z*).

35. (*a*) Structure *A* shows a secretory vesicle which buds off from the *trans* side of the Golgi complex after the secretory proteins are processed, it will fuse with the plasma membrane and release its contents into the extracellular space.

36. (*a*) *A*–Vacuole, these are storage sacs for solids or liquids such as amino acids, sugars, organic acid and some protein.
B–The secretory vesicle contains hormones which needs to be transported from one cell to other.
C–Cisternae, these are flattened memberane, sac-like structures that are an integral part of packaging and modification processes of proteins.

37. (*c*) *A*–Leucoplast, *B*–Any colour (except green). Leucoplasts are the colourless pigments which store starch, oils and protein granules. They are found in non-photosynthetic tissues of plants. On the other hand the chromoplasts contain any colour pigment (except green) and impart colours to the petals of the plant/flower.

38. (*b*) The correct match is as follows

A.	Cell wall	2.	Security guard of the cell as it protect the cell from external environment.
B.	Nucleus	1.	Head quarter of the cell as it controls functioning of the cell.
C.	Endoplasmic reticulum	5.	Channel for transportation and detoxification.
D.	Chloroplast	3.	Kitchen of the cell as it contains chlorophyll which involve in photosynthesis process.
E.	Golgi body	6.	Packaging of product and formation of lysosome.
F.	Lysosome	4.	Suicidal bags as it contains hydrolytic enzymes.

39. (*c*) The correct option is 'c' as
Meiosis produces four daughter cells and it is helpful in sexual reproduction as it forms male and female gametes.
Meiosis results in four unique daughter cells.
The incorrect statement can be corrected as mitasis occurs in the autosomes and the chromosome number remains same as that of parent. In meiosis, chromosome number reduced to half.

Tissues

1. (*d*) Sugarcane possesses intercalary meristem at the nodes of stems which can divide and form new cells.

2. (*a*) A is to be identified as optical meristem, which is present at the tip of roats, shoots and their branches.

3. (*b*) Mary made the correct statement as,
The vascular cambium produce new xylem and phloem each year and as a result the trunk, branches and root continue to increase in diameter.
More older the tree more will be the diameter of that tree.

4. (*c*) Apical meristem (*P*) is present at the growing tips of stems and roots. The girth of stem and root increases due to lateral meristem (*R*). Intercalary meristem (*Q*) present at the base of the leaves or internodes on twig.

5. (*a*) The given diagram shows surface view of leaf which consists of epidermal cells, stomata and guard cell.
A—Stomata
B—Guard cell
C—Epidermal cell

6. (*b*) The meristem is known as dividing tissue, if we cut the meristem, the plant growth is stopped.

7. (*a*) Both A and R are true and R is the correct explanation of A. Intercalary meristem increases the length of plant like apical meristem as it originates from the apical meristem.

8. (*a*) Vessels are multicellular tube-like structures with wide lumen found in xylem of plants and help in the conduction of water and minerals.

9. (*b*) Both A and R are true, but R is not the correct explanation of A. It can be corrected as xylem is a complex tissue because it is made up of more than one type of cells. It consists of tracheids, vessels, xylem parenchyma and xylem fibres.

10. (*d*) Xylem vessels are very long tube-like structures formed by a row of cells placed end to end. The transverse walls between these cells are partially or completely dissolved to form continuous water channels.

11. (*b*) The correct option is b,
A represents sieve tubes. These are tubular cells with perforated walls. Companion cell (c) is a parenchymatous cells. *B* is phloem parenchyma. It has cylindrical shape with dense cytoplasm.

12. (*c*)

13. (*c*) Statements I and IV are incorrect and can be corrected as
Root hairs on epidermal cells increase the total absorptive surface area and helps in absorption. Suberin makes cork cells impervious to gases and water.

14. (*b*) *A*—Primary, because cell wall of collenchyma is made up of cellulose and pectin.
B—Lignin, because cell wall of sclerenchyma is made up of lignin, which make thick wall.
C—Living, collenchyma are made up of living cells.

15. (*a*)

16. (*a*) The given diagram is of simple squamous epithelial tissue, which is found in the inner lining of mouth, oesophagus, blood vessels and covering of the tongue.

17. (*c*) Cuboidal epithelium is present in the tubular parts of nephron. These cells often form microvilli to increase the absorptive surface area of cell. In respiratory tract, cilliated ipithelium tissues are present.

Glandular epithelium tissues are found in breast, lung stomach. Squamous epithelium are present in kidney and resperatory tract.

18. (*d*) While doing work and running, skeletal muscles contract and pull the tendon (which connects muscles to bones) to move the bone.

19. (*b*) Ligaments connects one bone with another. In case of dislocation of bones, ligament breakage take place.

20. (*c*) *A*—Bone as it shows osteocyte.
B—Cartilage as it show chondrocytes.

21. (*c*) *A*—Granulocytes
B—Agranulocytes

Granulocytes and agranulocytes are two types of WBCs. found in blood. Granulocytes contains numerous granules in the cytoplasm and their nuclei are lobed, e.g. neutrophils, basophils and eosinophils, whereas, agranulocytes have few or no granules in the cytoplasm and have a large spherical nucleus, e.g. lymphocytes and monocytes.

22. (*b*) In the given figures
A–RBC
B–Basophils
C–Eosinophils
D–Neutrophils
E–Monocytes
F–Platelets

23. (*d*) RBC contains haemoglobin, WBC is integral part of immune system that help in fighting diseases by producing antibodies and engulfing the germs and pathogen. Platelets help in the clotting of blood. Plasma is the largest part of our blood.

24. (*c*) Both smooth and cardiac muscles are involuntary in nature. Paralysis is a loss of strength and control over skeletal muscles which are voluntary in nature is

25. (*b*) Columnar epithelium.
Specialised for absorption and has cilia or microvilli. These cells are found in the lining of stomach and intestine.

26. (*b*) *A*—Xylem, *B*—Vascular bundle, *C*—Phloem

Xylem and phloem constitute to form vascular bundle, they are complex tissues as they are made up of more than one type of cells. They helps in transportation of water and food, respectively in plants.

Vascular bundle is characteristic feature of plants only. They are not present in animals.

27. (*a*)

28. (*a*) Fibrous cartilage-contain more collagen-Intervertebral disc.
Elastic cartilage-contain both collagen and elastin fibres Epiglottis elastin fibres that is present is the epiglottis.

29. (*d*) The given Venn diagram show types of parenchyma. '*A*' represents parenchyma permanent tissue which have living cells and generally stores food.

In some situations, parenchyma contain chlorophyll and perform photosynthesis and then is called chlorenchyma (*B*).

In aquatic plants, large air cavities are present in parenchyma to help them float. Such type of parenchyma is called aerenchyma (*C*).

30. (*c*) Cutin is a wax like, water repellent material that is present on the surface of the plant. It has waterproof quality.

Suberin is present in cork cells that makes them impervious to gases and water.

Lignin is a hard substance with great tensile and compressional strength. It is present in the cell wall of sclerenchyma cells.

Cellulose is a polymer of glucose. It is the most significant structural component of plant cell wall.

31. (*b*) The skeletal muscles are voluntary and not involuntary and are straitedin nature.

Cardiac muscle is found only in the heart and involuentary in nature.

The smooth muscles are not straited.

32. (*a*) 1-Red blood corpuscles
2- White blood corpuscles
3- Platelets
4- Blood plasma

Motion

1. (*c*) Since, average speed $= \dfrac{\text{Total distance}}{\text{Total time}}$
The required average speed for the rest of the journey $= \dfrac{75}{2 - 0.5 - 0.25} = 60\ \text{km/h}$

2. (*b*) At the instant when ball *A* passes ball *B*, it has the same position and acceleration as ball *B*. As after the kick only gravity is working as force on both balls.

3. (*c*) In the absence of air resistance on the Moon, the acceleration of both coin and feather are the same. Hence, they fall together.
In the presence of air resistance on Earth, the lighter feather will reach terminal velocity first. The terminal velocity of coin will be higher as the coin is heavier.
The feather will take a longer time to cover the same height with a smaller speed.

4. (*d*) Distance travelled
= Area under the speed-time graph
= Area of trapezium
$= \dfrac{1}{2}(10 + 20)\, 40 = 600\ \text{m}$

5. (*c*) The car is first at rest (slope is zero, horizontal line). The car then moves with increasing non-uniform acceleration (slope varies with a curve).
Finally, it moves with a uniform acceleration (slope is constant, a straight line). The speed increases uniformly as time increases.

6. (*d*) In circular motion, the velocity is always changing as the direction is always changing. Hence, due to change in velocity, an acceleration is produced towards its centre called centripetal acceleration. This acceleration is due to centripetal force directed towards centre.

7. (*b*) Angular velocity,
$$\omega = \frac{\theta}{t} \quad \ldots [\because 1\ \text{h} = 3600\ \text{sec}]$$
$$= \frac{2\pi}{3600} = \frac{\pi}{1800}\ \text{rad/s}$$

8. (*d*) Since, force is always perpendicular to the body, work done by it will be zero.
So, kinetic energy is constant.
Also, velocity is constant in magnitude but direction of velocity is changing at every point.
Hence, magnitude of acceleration is constant.
It is the case of circular motion.

9. (*a*) For an electron revolving around the atomic nucleus the necessary centripetal force is provided by electrostatic force of attraction between the electron and the protons in the nucleus.

10. (*a*) For the first time, $75 = \dfrac{1}{2} \times 10 \times t^2$
$$\Rightarrow \quad t^2 = \frac{75}{5} = 15$$
$$\therefore \quad t = 3.8\ \text{s}$$
For second time, $80 = \dfrac{1}{2} \times 10 \times t^2$
$$\therefore \quad t = 4\ \text{s}$$
Hence, time of exposure is $= 4 - 3.8$
$= 0.2$ s.

11. (*c*) For motion from *P* to *Q*,
$$y = \frac{1}{2} g t_1^2 \quad \ldots\text{(i)}$$
For motion from *P* to *R*,
$$2y = \frac{1}{2} g (t_1 + t_2)^2 \quad \ldots\text{(ii)}$$
From Eqs. (i) and (ii), we get
$$2t_1^2 = (t_1 + t_2)^2$$
$$\Rightarrow \quad t_1 + t_2 = \sqrt{2}\, t_1$$
$$\Rightarrow \quad t_1(\sqrt{2} - 1) = t_2$$
$$\Rightarrow \quad \frac{t_1}{t_2} = \frac{1}{\sqrt{2} - 1}$$

12. (*c*) Time taken to drop a body from a height is independent of its mass.
$$t = \sqrt{\frac{2h}{g}} \Rightarrow t \propto \sqrt{h}$$
$$\Rightarrow \quad \frac{t_1}{t_2} = \sqrt{\frac{a}{b}}$$
$$\Rightarrow \quad t_1 : t_2 = \sqrt{a} : \sqrt{b}$$

13. (*a*) The first stone and second stone will possess same velocity *u* during their downward journey from the roof of the building. They are acted upon by the same gravitation acceleration. Therefore, they will strike the ground with the same velocity.

14. (*b*) Since, $s = ut + \dfrac{1}{2} g t^2$ and $u = 0$
$$\therefore \quad s = \frac{1}{2} g t^2 \Rightarrow s \propto t^2$$

$\Rightarrow \quad \frac{s_1}{s_2} = \frac{t_1^2}{t_2^2}$

$\Rightarrow \quad \frac{20}{5} = \frac{2^2}{t_2^2}$

$\Rightarrow \quad t_2^2 = 2^2 \times \frac{5}{20}$

$\therefore \quad t_2 = 1$ s

15. (*d*) Given, $v = \sqrt{50 - 8x}$

$\Rightarrow \quad v^2 = 50 - 8x$

Comparing with the equation

$v^2 = u^2 + 2as$, we get

$2a = -8$

$\Rightarrow \quad a = -4 \text{ m/s}^2$

16. (*d*) $s = ut + \frac{1}{2}at^2$

$\because \quad u = 0 \Rightarrow s = \frac{1}{2}at^2$

Since, a is constant, so $s \propto t^2$.

$\Rightarrow \quad \frac{s_1}{s_2} = \frac{t_1^2}{t_2^2}$

$\Rightarrow \quad \frac{s_1}{s_2} = \frac{t_1^2}{(2t_1^2)} = \frac{t_1^2}{4t_1^2}$

$\Rightarrow \quad s_2 = 4s_1$

17. (*c*) The motion of the Earth around the Sun requires same force of attraction between them. The gravitational force between them provides the necessary centripetal force for Earth's motion around Sun.

18. (*d*) Given, $v = 8 - 0.01t$

Comparing with the equation $v = u + at$

We get $\quad a = -0.01 \text{ m/s}^2$

$\therefore$ Retardation $= 0.01 \text{ m/s}^2$

19. (*d*) $s_n = u + a\left[n - \frac{1}{2}\right]$.

For a freely falling body,

$u = 0$ and $a = +g$

$\therefore \quad s_1 : s_2 : s_3 = g\left[1 - \frac{1}{2}\right] : g\left[2 - \frac{1}{2}\right] : g\left[3 - \frac{1}{2}\right]$

$= \frac{1}{2} : \frac{3}{2} : \frac{5}{2} = 1 : 3 : 5$

20. (*c*) II. As, $s = ut + \frac{1}{2}at^2$

$$s = 0 + \frac{1}{2}at^2 \text{ or } t = \sqrt{\frac{2s}{a}} \Rightarrow t \propto \sqrt{s}$$

Given, $s_1 : s_2 = 3 : 5$

$\therefore \quad t_1 : t_2 = \sqrt{3} : \sqrt{5}$

IV. All bodies fall with same acceleration (g).

V. Time of flight is independent of the mass of the bodies.

21. (*c*) Slope of the line gives the speed of the body. Therefore, speed of cars is in the following order.

Speed of $C >$ Speed of $D >$ Speed of $A >$ Speed of B.

Force and Laws of Motion

1. (*d*) While opening a tap two parallel , opposite and equal forces acts at the point.

2. (*c*) The force applied on an inflated balloon will either burst the ballon, change the position or the shape of the balloon.

3. (*a*) The weight of an object is given by $w = mg$. Since, mass remains constant. So, change in gravity will affect the weight of an object.

4. (*a*) As ball C is the deepest, it has the greatest impact and hence the greatest mass.

5. (*a*) Only statement II is true. Box A will be lifted only when the upward force applied is more than the weight of the box. The gravitational forces acting on both the boxes are same.

6. (*c*) As the objects in option (*c*) are moving in a straight line path, so they are subjected to a balanced external force.

7. (*c*) The patch of oil decreases the frictional force between the tyres and the dry road. Time taken to slow down the car on road B increases, because of the decrease in frictional force (resistive force).

8. (*c*) The shock absorber follows Newton's third law of motion, i.e. for every shock (action) they give equal and opposite reaction and hence, saves the vehicle from getting the direct shock or jerk.

9. (*b*) According to Newton's first law, the water in the tank would tend to remain in motion even after the brakes are applied. So, the water in the tank would move forward.

10. (*d*) Using Newton's third law, the same spring force pulls on both trolleys. Let mass of X and Y be $2m$ and m, respectively.

Force on X = Force on Y

$\therefore \quad 2m \times 2\text{m/s}^2 = m \times a \Rightarrow a = 4 \text{ m/s}^2$

where, a is the initial acceleration of Y.

11. (a) Using Newton's first law, the 20 kg is at rest and there is no resultant force because the weight of body is balanced by the tension in rope.

12. (b) Using Newton's second law,
$$54 - F = ma$$
$$\Rightarrow \quad F = 54 - ma$$
$$= 54 - (6 \times 6) = 18\text{ N}$$

13. (b) According to Newton's third law, the magnitude of the force exerted by astronaut A on astronaut B is equal to the force exerted by B on A.

14. (a) The force will be zero when acceleration is zero. For region AB and CD, velocity will be uniform and hence acceleration will be zero.

15. (c) Given, $m = 200\text{ g} = 0.2\text{ kg}$
$u = 15\text{ ms}^{-1}$, $v = 25\text{ ms}^{-1}$,
$t = 2.5\text{s}$ and $F =$ constant
$$\text{Force, } F = ma = m\left(\frac{v-u}{t}\right) = 0.2\left[\frac{25-15}{2.5}\right]$$
$$= 0.2 \times \frac{10}{2.5} = \frac{20}{25} = 0.8\text{ N}$$

16. (b) Newton's third law of motion is applicable in all situation whether the bodies are in motion or at rest.

17. (c) Given, mass of object, $m = 4$ kg
$F = -10$N (minus sign for opposite direction of force)
$$\text{Acceleration, } a = \frac{F}{m} = \frac{-10}{4} = -2.5\text{ m/s}^2$$
The position of object is given as
$$x = ut + \frac{1}{2}at^2$$
$$= 20 \times 2 + \frac{1}{2}(-2.5) \times 2^2$$
$$= 40 - 5 = 35\text{ m}$$

18. (a) Given, $m = 200\text{ g} = 0.2\text{ kg}$
$u = 4\text{ m/s}$, $v = 2u = 2 \times 4 = 8\text{ m/s}$
$F = 10\text{ N}$
Acceleration on the object
$$a = \frac{F}{m} = \frac{10}{0.2} = 50\text{ m/s}^2$$
$\therefore$ Position of object after, $t = 20$ s
$$s = ut + \frac{1}{2}at^2 = 4 \times 20 + \frac{1}{2} \times 50 \times 20^2 = 10.08\text{ km}$$

19. (d) For, $t < 0$ and $t > 6$ s, the position of the body is not changing, i.e. body is at rest. So, no force is acting on the body in these intervals.
For, $0 < t < 6$ s, the position of body continuously changing with uniform rate as the position time graph is straight line. Thus, acceleration, $a = 0$. Hence, no force acts on the body during this interval also. Thus,
$F_1 = F_2 = F_3 = 0$ N

20. (d)

21. (c) Weight of the book,
$$W = mg = 3 \times 10 = 30\text{ N}$$
Reaction force on the table
= Weight of the book on the table
= 30 N
Since, action and reaction acts in opposite direction on same line, hence angle between them will be 180°.

22. (b) As skate-board has wheel, so the friction is least and the force required is also least in case. Also, the force required in case of inclined plane is most. So, the force required is maximum in case D.
Force required in case A is less than B

23. (c) The weight of the can acts vertically downwards and do not affect the initial horizontal motion of the can. The ease of motion is dependent on the mass of can which is same on both the Earth and the Moon.

24. (b) Given, $m = 2$ kg

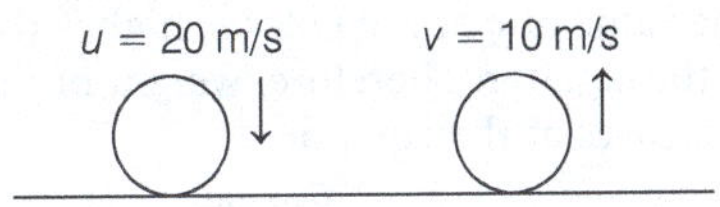

According to Newton's second law of motion,
$$F = \frac{\Delta p}{\Delta t} = \frac{m(v-u)}{\Delta t}$$
$$= \frac{2(10+20)}{0.04} \qquad [\because u = -20\text{ m/s}]$$
$$= \frac{60}{0.04} = 1500\text{ N}$$

25. (c) Since, the plane gains speed, it is accelerating. Using Newton's second law, there is a resultant horizontal force acting on the plane (i.e., $T > R$). Also because the aircraft is at a constant vertical height. Hence, the vertical forces are balanced (i.e., $L = W$).

26. (c) If two bodies of different masses move with the same momentum, then the heavier body will have lesser velocity.
The area under F-t graph gives impulse.

Gravitation

1. (*a*) Objects falling freely under gravity have constant acceleration,

Let acceleration on Moon, $a = g$

As, $v = u + at$

As object is falling, $v = u + gt$

If, $u = 0$

The two objects falling freely will have same velocity at any instant.

2. (*b*) The radius of Earth is maximum at the equator and minimum at the poles. Since, the value of acceleration due to gravity is inversely proportional to the square of radius (i.e. $g \propto R^{-2}$). So, the value of acceleration due to gravity is minimum at the equator and maximum on poles. Hence, it decreases from pole to equator.

3. (*a*) The weight of any object at the centre of the Earth is zero. Since, $g = 0$ at the centre of Earth.

4. (*b*) As, $F = \frac{Gm_1m_2}{r^2}$

Doubling the masses and keeping the distance same

$$F' = \frac{G(2m_1)(2m_2)}{r^2} = \frac{4G\,m_1m_2}{r^2} = 4F$$

5. (*c*) Weight $= mg \Rightarrow m \times 9.8 = 49\text{ N} \Rightarrow m = 5\text{ kg}$

The value of g at the poles is higher than that at the equator. Therefore, weight of the laptop decreases at the equator.

6. (*a*) As, we know, $F = \frac{Gm_1m_2}{r^2}$ and $r \simeq 1\text{ m}$

$$\therefore F \simeq \frac{6.67 \times 10^{-11} \times 60 \times 60}{(1)^2} \simeq 10^{-7}\text{ N}$$

7. (*a*) We know, $F = \frac{GMm}{R^2}$

$$F = \frac{6.67 \times 10^{-11} \times (1.67 \times 10^{-27})^2}{(10^{-15})^2}$$

$$= 18.60 \times 10^{-35} = 1.86 \times 10^{-34}\text{ N}$$

8. (*c*) Here, $F = \frac{GM_em_{sat}}{r^2}$

$$\therefore a = \frac{F}{m_{sat}} = \frac{GM_e}{r^2} \qquad [\because F = m_{sat}\,a]$$

$$= \frac{6.67 \times 10^{-11} \times 6 \times 10^{24}}{(44400 \times 10^3)^2} = 0.2\text{ ms}^{-2}$$

9. (*d*) As, we know, $w = mg$ and $g = \frac{GM}{R^2}$

$$\therefore w = \frac{GMm}{R^2} = G \times \frac{Mm}{R^2}$$

$$\frac{w'}{w_e} = \frac{m'}{M_e} \times \left[\frac{R_e}{R'}\right]^2 = \frac{2M_e}{M_e} \times \left[\frac{R_e}{3R_e}\right]^2 = \frac{2}{9}$$

$$\Rightarrow w' = \frac{2}{9}w_e = \frac{2}{9} \times 900 = 200\text{ N}$$

10. (*b*) We know $g = \frac{GM}{R^2}$

For the given body, $m = \frac{M}{2}$

and $r = \frac{R}{2}$

$$\therefore g' = \frac{Gm}{r^2} = \frac{GM}{2} \times \frac{4}{R^2}$$

$$g' = 2\frac{GM}{R^2}$$

$$\Rightarrow g' = 2g = 2 \times 9.8 = 19.6\text{ ms}^{-2}$$

11. (*c*) As, $g = \frac{GM}{R^2}$

$$\therefore g' = \frac{G(2M)}{(3R)^2} = \frac{2}{9}\frac{GM}{R^2} = \frac{2}{9}g$$

$$g' = \frac{2}{9} \times 9.8 = 2.17\text{ ms}^{-2}$$

Weight of the body on planet, $w' = mg'$

$= 5 \times 2.17 = 10.85\text{ N}$

12. (*b*) If $R' = 2R$, then $w' = \frac{GMm}{4R^2} = \frac{1}{4}w$

one-fourth of weight.

13. (*d*) As, $g = \frac{GM}{R^2} \Rightarrow M \propto gR^2$

$$\therefore \frac{M_e}{M_m} = \frac{9.8}{1.7} \times \frac{R_e^2}{(0.27\,R_e)^2} = \frac{9.8}{1.7 \times 0.27 \times 0.27} = 79$$

14. (*d*) Let, M_e and R_1 are the mass and radius of the Earth, g_1 is the acceleration due to gravity.

Taking, $g_1 = \frac{GM_e}{R_1^2}$ and $g_2 = \frac{GM_e}{R_2^2}$

Given, $R_2 = \frac{96}{100}R_1$

So, $g_2 = \frac{GM_e}{(0.96R_1)^2}$

Change in g is given by $\frac{g_1 - g_2}{g_1} \times 100$

$$= \frac{\frac{GM_e}{R_1^2} - \frac{GM_e}{(0.96R_1)^2}}{\frac{GM_e}{R_1^2}} \times 100$$

$$= \left[1 - \left(\frac{1}{0.96}\right)^2\right] \times 100 \approx 8\%$$

15. (*c*) G is a universal gravitational constant with value 6.67×10^{-11} Nm^2/kg^2.

16. (*d*) According to universal law of gravitation, the force of attraction acting between any two objects is always equal and opposite.
Hence, $F_1 = F_2$.

17. (*a*) As, $s = ut + \frac{1}{2}at^2$
Here, $u = 0$ as initially the object was at rest and $a = g$ as the object is falling freely

$$s = \frac{1}{2}gt^2 \Rightarrow t = \sqrt{\frac{2s}{g}}$$

s is same for both the ball and thus t will be same for both.

18. (*a*) Let m' be the mass of particle, which is placed at a distance x from A.

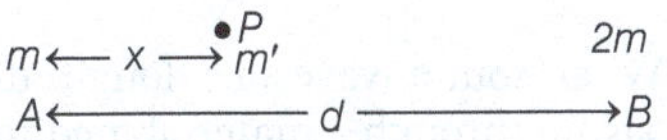

$$F_1 = \frac{Gmm'}{x^2} \text{ towards } A$$

$$F_2 = \frac{G(2m)m'}{(d-x)^2} \text{ towards } B$$

The net force $= 0$, if $F_1 = F_2$

$$\Rightarrow \frac{Gmm'}{x^2} = \frac{G(2m)m'}{(d-x^2)} \Rightarrow x = \frac{d}{1+\sqrt{2}}$$

19. (*c*) As, $w = mg$ and $g \propto \frac{1}{R^2} \Rightarrow w \propto \frac{1}{R^2}$

$\because \quad R_1 < R_2$

So, $\quad w_1 > w_2$

20. (*a*) $F = \frac{Gm_1m_2}{r^2}$

$$= \frac{6.67 \times 10^{-11} \times 1 \times 2}{(1)^2} = 1.33 \times 10^{-10} \text{ N}$$

(i) Acceleration of 1 kg body, $a = \frac{F}{m}$

$$= \frac{1.33 \times 10^{-10}}{1} = 1.33 \times 10^{-10} \text{ ms}^{-2}$$

(ii) Acceleration of 2 kg body

$$a = \frac{F}{m} = \frac{1.33 \times 10^{-10}}{2}$$

$$= 6.67 \times 10^{-11} \text{ ms}^{-2}$$

Work and Energy

1. (*b*) Work done, $W = F \cdot s$
Thus, for the positive work to be done on an object, a force must be applied and the object must move in the direction of force applied.

2. (*a*) Here, statement I is incorrect. Work done will be zero when the angle between force and displacement is 90°.

3. (*d*) Box Q did more work than Box P.
Here, work is done against gravitational force.

4. (*d*) In the given case, work is done by both the balls as there was a transfer of energy between them.

5. (*d*) Net force = 10 N – 5 N
F = 5 N, towards right
As, the ball will move towards right. So, work is said to be done.

6. (*b*) Here, force is perpendicular to the displacement.
$\therefore \quad W = F \times s \times \cos 90° = 0$

7. (*b*) Work done by the car is equal to the gain in gravitational potential energy of the car up the hill.
$\therefore$ Work done $= mgh = (500) \times (10) \times (10)$
$= 50000 \text{ J} = 5 \times 10^4 \text{ J}$

8. (*c*) $KE = \frac{1}{2}mv^2 \Rightarrow KE \propto v^2$
However, the mass of bullet is small and the velocity of bullet is very high. Therefore, KE of bullet is higher than KE of gun. i.e. $E_b > E_g$.

9. (*b*) From point A, the body is thrown upwards and hence it acquires KE and when it reaches the maximum height at point B, it acquires PE. Hence, according to law of conservation of energy. KE at A = PE at B.

10. (*c*) As the Nicole pedals, the dynamo spins and converts kinetic energy into electrical energy. The electrical energy is converted to heat and light energy in the bicycle by the lamp.

11. (*b*) The higher the potential energy, the deeper the impression made in sand. Both boxes have the same mass, but wooden box is at a greater height.
Hence, the wooden box has more PE and will make a deeper impression.

12. (*c*) Loss of KE = Work done = $F \cdot s$

Given that, both the retarding force F and KE are same for both lorry and car.

So, both the lorry and car would come to rest at the same distance.

13. (*a*) The amount of KE depends on its mass, since sand is continuously falling out of the bag, the total mass of the man at point B is less than his total mass at point A. Hence, his KE will be less at point B than at point A.

14. (*a*) As, energy is conserverd, so $mgh = \frac{1}{2}mv^2$

$$\Rightarrow v = \sqrt{2gh}$$

$$= \sqrt{2 \times 980 \times 10} = \sqrt{19600} \quad [\because g = 980 \text{ cms}^{-1}]$$

$$= 140 \text{ cms}^{-1}$$

$$= 1.4 \text{ ms}^{-1}$$

15. (*a*) Average power $= \frac{\text{Work done}}{\text{Time}}$

$$= \frac{F \times d}{t} = \frac{300 \times 3.0}{20} = 45 \text{ W}$$

16. (*c*) Power $= \frac{\text{Work done}}{\text{Time}} = \frac{\text{Force} \times \text{Distance}}{\text{Time}}$

$$= \frac{\text{Weight} \times \text{Distance}}{\text{Time}}$$

$$= \frac{500 \times 5}{10} = 250 \text{ W}$$

17. (*d*)Power $= \frac{\text{Work done}}{\text{Time}} = \frac{\text{Force} \times \text{Distance}}{\text{Time}}$

$$= \frac{(200)(10) \times (5)}{(24)(60)(60)} = 0.115 \text{ W}$$

18. (*b*) Average power output $= \frac{\text{Work done}}{\text{Time}}$

Total work done = Force × Distance × No. of push ups

$$= 300 \times 0.5 \times 10$$

Average power output $= \frac{1500}{30} = 50 \text{ W}$

19. (*d*) According to work-energy theorem,

$$W_{\text{net}} = \frac{1}{2} m (v_f^2 - v_i^2)$$

For O to A, $v_f > v_i$

⇒ Work done is positive.

For A to B, $v_f = v_i$

⇒ Work done is zero.

For B to C, $v_f < v_i$

⇒ Work done is negative.

For C to D, $v_f < v_i$

⇒ Work done is negative.

So, all the statements are incorrect.

20. (*b*) When a cyclist move on the road, the frictional force is in backward direction but the motion of cycle is in forward direction. So, the work done is negative.

$$W = F \cdot s = Fs \cos(-180°) = Fs$$

21. (*c*) Work done, $W = F \sin\theta \times s$

$$= mg \sin\theta \times s$$

$$= 20 \text{ kg} \times 10 \text{ ms}^{-2} \times 3 \sin 30°$$

$$= 20 \times 10 \times 3 \times (1/2) = 300 \text{ J}$$

22. (*c*) A battery converts chemical energy into electrical energy.

The decrease in the PE of a ball of mass 20 kg which falls from a height 25 cm is

$$\text{PE} = mgh = 20 \times 9.8 \times 25 \times 10^{-2} = 49 \text{ J}$$

When a car acceleration up a hill its kinetic energy decreases but its potential energy increases.

Sound

1. (*d*) When sound waves, i.e. longitudinal wave propagate through a material medium, then energy and momentum are transferred but mass does not get transmitted.

2. (*b*) If the particles of medium vibrate perpendicular to the direction of the propagation of wave, then such a wave is called transverse wave.

3. (*a*) Sound waves are longitudinal and have speed $\simeq$ 5000 m/s in solids.

3×10^8 m/s is the speed of light, which is the highest one.

4. (*c*) Elastic waves require a medium for their propagation like a sound wave.

While light wave, X-rays and radio waves do not require material medium because he are electromagnetic waves.

5. (*b*) Light and radio waves are examples of electromagnetic waves which are all transverse waves. Sound is an example of longitudinal wave.

6. (*d*) A vibrating body produces sound depending upon the frequency because audiable frequency range is 20Hz to 20 kHz.

7. (*b*) Transverse waves are X-rays, waves on a string and gamma rays as particles in them displaces perpendicular to wave motion. Longitudinal waves are ultrasonic waves and infrasonic waves, as particles of medium are displaced along wave motion.

8. (*d*) The loudness of sound produced depends on the force with which it is struck.

9. (*a*) Velocity of sound increases with increase in temperature of the medium. as $v \propto T$.
Thus, wavelength also changes with the change in temperature of the medium as $\lambda \propto v$.

10. (*d*) Sound is produced in given recorder when one or two holes are close and others are open. Hence, sound is not produced in statements I, II and IV.

11. (*b*) The pitch depends on frequency, i.e. larger the frequency, greater will be pitch. The loudness of a sound depends on its amplitude, i.e. larger the amplitude, louder will be the sound produced.
In trumpet, the sound produced is louder but pitch is low.

12. (*c*) The correct match is
Quality—Waveform
Loudness—Intensity
Pitch—Frequency

13. (*d*) A node is a point along standing wave where the wave has minimum amplitude. While antinodes are points where amplitude is maximum. Here, for given diagram all statements are correct.

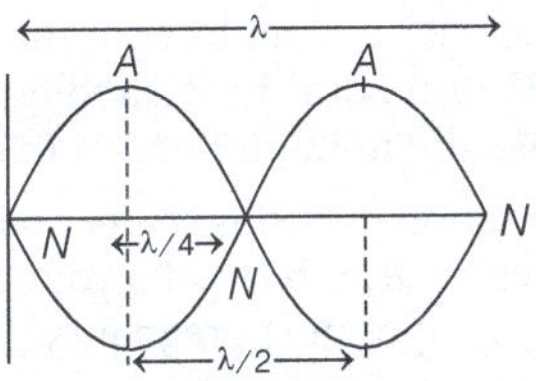

14. (*c*) Range of human audible frequencies is 20Hz to 20000Hz. Hence, option (*c*) represent the audible frequency range.

15. (*d*) Ultrasonic waves can be produced using galton whistle, piezoelectric oscillator and magnetostriction.

16. (*b*) Distance from wall $= \frac{v \cdot t}{2}$

$$= \frac{(330)(0.060)}{2} = 9.9\text{ m}$$

17. (*c*) The reflected wave would have a lower amplitude (since wall absorbs some of the sound energy). But same frequency, wavelength and speed and it has different velocity, since the direction of the wave has changed.

18. (*d*) Sound travels faster in solid than in air. So, boy and girl will hear the sound of train approaching through tracks before they could hear through air.

19. (*c*) Speed of sound in air increases with increase in humidity because, presence of moisture decreases the density of air. Due to change in the temperature of the medium, velocity of sound changes. Then is no transfer of heat from compression to rarefaction as air is a bad conductor of heat.

20. (*d*) In longitudinal waves, the particle of the medium oscillate parallel to the direction of propagation of wave.

21. (*b*) The correct match of given columns is
String vibration → Sitar
Membrane vibration → Tabla
Vibration of air column → Flute
Vibration of plate → Bicycle bell

22. (*b*) Let the aircraft and the submarine be x m above and below the tanker, respectively. Time taken by sound to reach the aircraft is

$$t_{\text{air}} = \frac{x}{340}\text{ s}$$

Time taken by sound to reach the submarine

$$t_{\text{water}} = \frac{x}{1520}\text{ s}$$

$$\text{Ratio of the time taken} = \frac{t_{\text{air}}}{t_{\text{water}}} = \frac{(x/340)}{(x/1520)}$$

$$= \frac{1520}{340} = 4.47$$

Improvement in Food Resources

1. (*c*) 'Rust of wheat' is an air-borne disease that attack on all aerial parts of the plants.

2. (*a*) Paddy crop require lot of water and fish culture can be done in combination with rice crop.

3. (*c*) Complete sentences are as follow

(i) **Black gram** is a protein yielding pulse. These are the crops that fulfill the protein requirement of our body.

(ii) **Rabi crops** are grown from November-April. They are grown in winter season, e.g. wheat, gram, etc.

(iii) **Nitrogen, phosphorus, potassium, calcium, magnesium and sulphur** are all macronutrients. They are required in large quantities by the plants.

(iv) **Organic farming** is a farming system with minimal or no use of chemicals and maximum input of organic manure. This farming method involves the use of biofertilisers and healthy cropping system.

(v) **Pesticides** include insecticides, herbicides and fungicides. These chemicals are sprayed on crop plants to protect them from insect pests.

4. (*d*) Integrated farming or Integrated agriculture implies a combination of agriculture with other forms of culture such as pisciculture, aquaculture, apiculture, sericulture, poultry farming, piggery, livestock production, etc.

5. (*d*) Excess irrigation of field leads to water logging of soil. It affect soil aeration and hence, plant roots do not grow properly. It increases salinity of soil and lead to soil erosion by washing away the top most layer of soil containing humus.

6. (*b*) Growing two or more crops on the same field is called mixed cropping.

7. (*b*) Sustainable agriculture can be defined as the adoption of various farming and production management techniques to maximise agricultural yield. Implementing such practices would help in (i) conserving natural resources, (ii) maintaining environmental balance and (iii) Coping with changing human needs.

8. (*b*) In intercropping, two or more crops are grown simultaneously on the same field in a definite pattern. A few rows of one crop alternate with a few rows of other crop.

9. (*b*) Statements II and III are incorrect and can be corrected as

In intercropping of each crop is harvested without much difficulty and it involves growing of two or more crops in separate strips. Rest all statements are correct.

10. (*a*) *A. mellifera* is the Italian bee that has been brought in India to increase the yield of honey.

11. (*b*) Harry made the correct statement as Photoperiods are related to the duration of sunlight and affects growth of plants and flowering of plant. Whereas photosynthesis is a process of making food by plants.

12. (*b*) Gangas-5 is a variety of maize. Kasturi is a variety of Basmati rice, has a high yield potential and is an excellent milling quality rice. Green manure prepared by composting green plant, so it is also called as bio-fertilisers. The Brown Swiss is an American breed of cattle.

13. (*c*) Maize (*P*) and wheat (*Q*) provide us carbohydrates for energy requirement therefore, known as energy giving food. Out of them, maize is a kharif crop grows in rainy season and wheat is rabi crop grows in winter season.

14. (*d*) Pisciculture is the culturing of fish. This culture is sometimes done in combination with a rice crop.

15. (*a*) "Seeds" in fish farming refers to the eggs of the fish. These are fertilised cells, which give birth to new young ones.

16. (*d*) Both A and R are false and can be corrected as Large schools of fish are can be located using satellites and echo-sounders. This helps in increasing the yield as large number of fish can be caught at the same time. Radio signals are not used for catching fish.

17. (*c*) Fertilisers mainly supply nitrogen (N), phosphorus (P) and potassium (K) to the plants.

18. (*a*) Cattle feed includes roughage and concentrates which are largely fibre and rich in protein level, respectively.

19. (*c*) *X* is an exotic or foreign breed which is selected for long lactation periods, while *Y* is a local breed that show-excellent resistance to disease. The two can be cross-breed to get animal with both the desired qualities, so as to increase the milk production in cattle farming.

20. (*c*) Lactation period is the period of milk production after birth of a young one, lasting generally upto next pregnancy.

21. (*a*) Both A and R are true and R is the correct explanation of A.

Dr. V Kurien is known as the father of white revolution because his idea on operation flood, made diary farming India's largest self-sustaining industry and the largest rural employment sector providing a income of all rural households..

22. (*d*) Both A and R are false and can be corrected as

Honeybees help farmers as they are pollinators of many crop species. Bees do not destroy the crops rather suck the nectar from the flower and make honey from it, which is food for them.

23. (*c*) Poultry feeds has a higher level of vitamins-A and K. Vitamin-K plays a key role in helping the blood to clot, preventing excessive bleeding. Vitamin-A is required for the proper development and functioning of eyes, skin, immune system and many other parts of body.

24. (*a*) *P*—Milch animal and *Q*—Drought animal. Milch animals helps in milk production e.g. cow, goat, etc. Drought animals helps in ploughing, irrigation, tilting, etc., e.g. donkey, bull, etc.

25. (*a*) Milk production is meagre in our country despite a large population of cattle. This is because of poor quality of feed given to them. Also, cattle suffer from many diseases due to lack of proper hygiene in housing.

26. (*c*) *A*—Meat production
B—Milk production
C—Agricultural work
All are the purposes for which cattle husbandry is done.

27. (*d*) Silver revolution is related to the increase in the production of egg.

28. (*b*) Pesticides are toxic for target pests and other organisms. They also create environmental pollution. An alternative practice is organic farming, an environment-friendly practice. It uses fertilisers, pesticides, etc., in minimal amount.

29. (*d*) Artificial insemination is the process of collecting sperm cells from a male animal and manually depositing them into the reproductive tract of a female. It is done in following sequences. The semen of healthy and tough animal is collected. It is preserved by freezing or chemical method. It is then injected into female reproductive tract during fertility period.

30. (*b*) Mericulture is culture of marine fishes for commercial use. Aquaculture is refer to cultivation of aquatic products under controlled condition. Capture fishing is catching fish from natural resources. Apiculture is culturing of bees for the production of honey and wax.

31. (*d*) The fish species can be stocked in paddy field. This is refer to as paddy-cum-fish culture.

32. (*c*) Green revolution that involves high production of food grains. Yellow revolution involves increased production of edible oils. Blue revolution include enhanced fish production, white revolution is increased milk production. Golden revolution is increased pulses production.

33. (*c*)

34. (*b*) The daily requirement or the ration for broilers is protein rich diet with adequate fat. The level of vitamin-A and vitamin-K is kept high in the poultry feeds.

35. (*a*) Statement II can be corrected as
Broiler and layer requires different housing, nutritional and environmental facilities. Rest all the statements are correct.

36. (*b*) Catla are surface feeders whereas, Rohu feed in central zone and mrigal are common carps found in bottom and surface of the pond. Pisciculture is culture of fish.

37. (*c*) Brown Swiss and Jersey are exotic breed of cattles, Leghorn is exotic breed of poultry. Whereas Red Sindhi and Sahiwal are local breed of cattles and Aseel is local/indigenous breed of poultry.

38. (*c*) The percent of protein content in milk is 4%, egg is 13% and fish is 19%.

39. (*d*) Fumigation is done to protect harvested crops from pests and insects as a preventive and control measures that is used before grains are stored for future use. Whereas, vaccination is given to farm animals to protect them from diseases caused by various bacteria and viruses. Fumigation using chemical helps in protection of crops against various pests.

40. (*d*)

Practice Set 1

1. (*d*) $\text{Speed} = \frac{\text{Distance}}{\text{Time}} = \frac{120\,\text{m}}{2\,\text{s}} = 60\ \text{ms}^{-1}$

Since, car is moving with a uniform speed. Hence, time taken by car,

$$\text{Time} = \frac{\text{Distance}}{\text{Speed}} = \frac{240\ \text{m}}{60\ \text{ms}^{-1}}$$

$\Rightarrow \quad t = 4\ \text{s}$

2. (*c*) Simple epithelium tissue is composed of a single layer of cell which rest on the basal lamena. These are comented to one another. This epithelium, lives the body cavities, tubes and ducts helping in diffusion, absorption, felteration and secretion.

3. (*c*) In CaO, valency of each of the constituent element is 2 and is equal to the total number of atoms present in one molecule of the compound.

4. (*d*) A body will float in equilibrium, if the centre of gravity and centre of buoyancy lie along the same line and weight of body is equal to weight of the liquid displaced by whole volume of the body.

5. (*d*) Radius of atom represented as the Earth, $r = 6.4 \times 10^6$ m

Let, the radius of the nucleus be x m.

According to the question,

$$\frac{r}{x} = 10^5 \Rightarrow x = \frac{r}{10^5}$$

$$\Rightarrow \quad x = \frac{6.4 \times 10^6}{10^5} \Rightarrow x = 64 \text{ m}$$

Thus, size of the nucleus would be 64 m.

6. (*b*) $1 \text{ N} = 10^5$ dyne

$$1 \text{ m} = 100 \text{ cm}$$

$$1 \text{ Nm}^{-2} = 10^5 \text{ dyne} \times (100)^{-2} \text{cm}^{-2}$$

$$= 10^5 \times 10^{-4} \text{ dyne cm}^{-2}$$

$$= 10 \text{ dyne cm}^{-2}$$

$$1 \text{ kg} = 1000 \text{ g} \Rightarrow 1 \text{ g} = 10^{-3} \text{ kg}$$

$$1 \text{ N} = 10^5 \text{ dyne}$$

$$1 \text{ g wt.} = 1g \times (g')$$

Where g' is acceleration due to gravity,

$$g' = 9.8 \text{ ms}^{-2}$$

$$1 \text{ N} = 1 \text{ kg ms}^{-2}$$

$$1\text{g wt.} = (10^{-3}) \text{ kg} \times 9.8 \text{ ms}^{-2} = 9.8 \times 10^{-3}\text{N}$$

$$= 9.8 \times 10^{-3} \times 10^5 \text{ dyne}$$

$$1 \text{ g wt.} = 980 \text{ dyne}$$

$$1 \text{ N} = 1 \text{ kg ms}^{-2}$$

kg fm^2, Here, f represents force. It is called kilogram force per square meter.

$$f = 9.8 \text{ ms}^{-2}$$

$$\text{Thus, } 1 \text{ kg fm}^{-2} = 1\text{kg} \times 9.8 \text{ ms}^{-2} \times \text{m}^{-2}$$

$$= 9.8 \text{ Nm}^{-2} = 9.8 \text{ Pascal}$$

$$1 \text{ kg fm}^{-2} = 9.8 \text{ Pa} \approx 10 \text{ Pa}$$

7. (*d*) The air used by scuba divers for breathing has the composition, 56% N_2, 32% O_2 and 11% He. To avoid bends as well as the toxic effects of high concentration of nitrogen in the blood.

8. (*b*) Material which is suitable as a heat shield, must have higher melting point than that of the space capsule and poorly conduct heat. In order to prevent getting hot and melt by the action of heat.

9. (*b*) According to the law of conservation of mass, Mass of reactants = Mass of products.

$$5.6 \text{ g} + 1.2 \text{ g} = 6.8 \text{ g of ammonia.}$$

$$N_2 = 5.6 \text{ g } H_2 = 1.2 \text{ g}$$

10. (*c*) The crap of pea would require a minimum quantity of NPK or urea because pea is a dicot and its roots contain nitrogen fixing bacteria in root nodules.

11. (*c*)

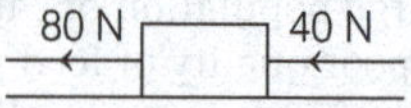

This pair of forces causes the greatest acceleration because the maximum force applied on only one direction.

12. (*b*) Electronic configuration of $X(8) = 2, 6$

Electronic configuration of $Y(17) = 2, 8, 7$

Both require electrons to complete their octet, so both are non-metals.

13. (*c*) The solution or water in bowl is hypotonic, so water enters in the grapes, this process is known as endosmosis.

14. (*a*) Mass of television (m) = 5 kg

height (h) = 1 m and $g = 10 \text{ m/s}^2$

Work is done by the person when a television of mass 5 kg is lifted from the ground. Which is stored as potential energy.

$\therefore$ Work done = Potential energy = mgh

$$= 5 \times 10 \times 1 = 50 \text{ J}$$

15. (*b*) As atomic mass of sulphur is 32.

Mass of sulphur in 10 g of sample

$$\frac{\text{Atomic Mass of S} \times \text{No. of atoms of S in sample}}{\text{Mass of one mole / g of sample}} \times 10\text{g}$$

Formula of sulphide	Mass of S in 10 g sample
NiS	$\frac{32}{90} \times 10 = 3.5\text{g}$
FeS_2	$\frac{2 \times 32}{120} \times 10 = 5.3\text{g}$
MoS_2	$\frac{2 \times 32}{160} \times 10 = 4 \text{ g}$
PbS	$\frac{32}{239} \times 10 = 1.3\text{g}$

$\therefore$ FeS_2 contain greatest mass of S.

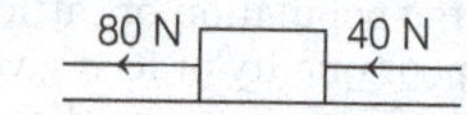

16. (*d*) When a patient is diagnosed with a viral infection, he/she should took antiviral medicines to treat himself. Penicillin is used to treat certain infections caused by bacteria. Deoxycyline is a broad spectrum tetracycline antibiotic that fights harmful bacteria in body.

17. (*a*) Let, the length of the train = l m

Speed of train $= 90 \text{ km/h} = 90 \times \frac{5}{18}$

$= 25 \text{ m/sec}$

Total distance covered by train in 60 sec

$= 600 + l$

Total distance = speed of train × time taken

$$600 + l = 25 \times 60$$
$$600 + l = 1500$$
$$l = 1500 - 600$$
$$\Rightarrow \quad l = 900 \text{ m}$$

So, length of train = 900 m.

18. (*a*) All the cells of the body obtain energy from the food that we eat. In the cytoplasm of a cell, the biochemical miniature factories called mitochondria which oxidises the food and release energy.

19. (*d*) Ablative protection is not used on the nose cones of passenger aircraft because the heat shield would disturb the aerodynamics of the passenger aircraft.

20. (*a*) Electron is a subatomic particle which is moving in orbitals, around the nucleus. It is responsible for the chemical properties of the elements.

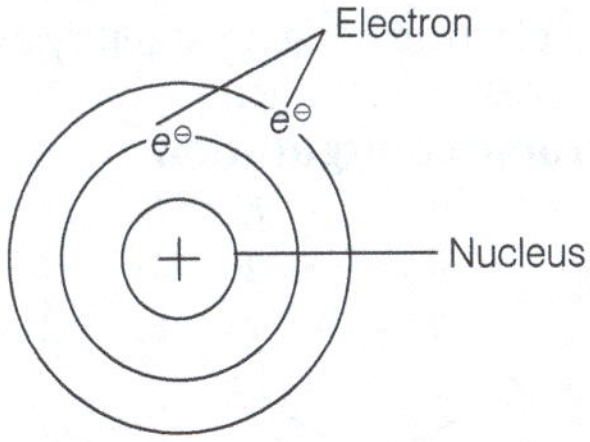

21. (*b*) A goal keeper in football pulls his hands backwards after holding the ball shot at the goal, this enables the goal keeper to reduce the force exerted by the ball on hands.

22. (*b*) Columnar epithelium farms the lining of small intestine, stomach and colen which pushes the mucus forward.

23. (*a*) $m = 1000$ kg

Submarine sinks in water with a uniform speed so,

$$a = 0$$

Force exerted on the submarine

$$F = m \cdot a$$
$$F = 1000 \times 0$$
$$\Rightarrow \quad F = 0$$

24. (*b*) When a mixture, in which the substances are regularly suspended in fluid, is called colloidal solution. A colloid is a very tiny and small material that is spread out uniformly all through another substance.

25. (*b*) *A* is the cytoplasm. It is the space present between the plasma membrane and the nucleus. It is filled by an amorphous, translucent, homogeneous, colloidal liquid. It consists of various inorganic molecules, such as 90% water, 7% proteins, 2% carbohydrates and lipids and 1% inorganic materials, minerals, vitamins, etc.

26. (*c*) Given, mass of water, $m = 180$ kg,

time, $t = 1$ hour

$= 60 \times 60$ s

Depth, $h = 6$ m

$$\therefore \text{Useful power, } P = \frac{mgh}{t} = \frac{180 \times 10 \times 6}{60 \times 60} = 3 \text{ W}$$

27. (*a*) Fruit cutting is a physical change because no new substance is formed when fruit is cut and stars twinkle due to atmospheric refraction. Twinkling of stars occurs since light passes through many different layers. Hence, it is not a chemical change.

28. (*c*) In case, the mechanical wave is transverse in nature, then the particles of the medium will move in X-axis. If the wave is longitudinal in nature, then the particles will move in Y-axis.

29. (*c*) Y is a plasma membrane or cell membrane of animal cell, which controls the movement of substances in and out of the cell.

30. (*b*) Power (P) = 2 kW = 2000 W

height (h) = 20 m

$\Rightarrow \quad g = 10 \text{ m/sec}^2$

time (t) = 1 min = 60 sec

$$\text{Power } (P) = \frac{mgh}{t}$$
$$2000 = \frac{m \times 10 \times 20}{60}$$
$$m = \frac{200 \times 6}{2}$$
$$\Rightarrow \quad m = 600 \text{ kg}$$

31. (*c*) In the given ionic species.
Fluoride ion $\rightarrow F^-$
Fluoride ion has 10 electrons and 10 neutrons.
Aluminium ion $\rightarrow Al^{+3}$
Aluminium has 13 electrons in neutral form, when it forms aluminium ion, then aluminium ion has only 10 electrons and 14 neutrons.
Oxide ion $\rightarrow O^{2-}$
Oxygen has 8 electrons in neutral form. When it forms oxide ion, then oxide ion has 10 electrons and 8 neutrons.
Sodium ion $\rightarrow Na^+$
Sodium ion has 10 electrons and 12 neutrons.
So, in all the given ion species, only oxide ion (O^{2-}) has more electrons than neutrons.

32. (*b*) Car *A* and car *C* are covering equal distances at equal interval of time. Hence, they have uniform velocity and zero acceleration. In case of car *B*, distance travelled is not equal at each time interval, hence, it is in non-uniformly accelerated motion.

33. (*b*) Iodine test is perform to show the presence of starch. It is indicated by blue-black or purple colour when starch is present and indicated by brown colour when starch is absent. This experiment tells that plants cells usually have parts that contain starch as plant cells give blue-black or purple colour on staining with iodine solution. Whereas animal cells do not contain any stored starch.

34. (*c*) Water molecules are showing osmosis. They are moving from outside to inside of the cell where there is high solute concentration. Osmosis is a special type of diffusion in which movement of the solvent occur through semi-permeable membrane from region of high concentration of solvent to region of low concentration of solvent. The solvent is usually water in case of osmosis.

35. (*b*) Here, speed, $s = 344 \text{ m/s}$
Time, $t = 10 \text{ s}$
Distance, $d = ?$

$$d = s \times t = 344 \times 10$$
$$= 3440 \text{ m} = 3.44 \text{ km}$$

36. (*a*) Cell *A* is a plant cell and cell *B* is an animal cell. Plant cell has cell wall in addition to plasma membrane, whereas animal cell has only plasma membrane. Plants can make their own food by the process of photosynthesis, whereas animals depends on plants and other animals for their food, i.e. they are heterotrophs. Plants have stomata that allow gaseous exchange, whereas stomata are absent in animals. Animal cells are round in shape, whereas plant cells are rectangular in shape.

37. (*c*) Loudness of a sound depends on the amplitude, while pitch of a sound depends on the frequency of the sound wave.

38. (*b*) Volume of gas at STP
$\Rightarrow$ no. of moles $\times \underbrace{22.4}_{(a)}$

- Number of moles
  $\Rightarrow$ Vol. of gas at STP $\div \underbrace{22.4}_{(b)}$
- Number of moles
  $\Rightarrow$ No. of molecules $\div \underbrace{N_A}_{(c)}$
- Number of molecules
  $\Rightarrow$ No. of moles $\times \underbrace{N_A}_{(d)}$

39. (*b*) Since, velocity time graph for a moving object is curved line, this means that object is moving with non-uniform accelerated motion, therefore body is moving with variable acceleration.

40. (*a*) *A* has 9 electrons and 9 protons, so its electronic configuration is (2, 7). It has 7 electrons in its outermost shell. So, it gains 1 electron in it's outermost shell for stability.
B has 12 electrons and 12 protons, so its electronic configuration is (2, 8, 2). It has 2 electrons in their outermost shell. So, it easily loses 2 electrons to gain stability and form cation with + 2 charge.

Electronic configuration

	K	*L*	*M*
A $\longrightarrow$	2,	7	
B $\longrightarrow$	2,	8,	2

Symbol *A* *B*

Charge −1 +2

Formula BA_2

41. (*a*) Peter does work. Work done by a force acting on an object is equal to the magnitude of the force multiplied by the distance moved in the direction of the force.
John is holding a box and the displacement of the box is zero.
Peter is lifting the box and doing a work which is equal to $w = mgh$.

It has to be noticed that gravity also does work in opposite direction which is equal to $-mgh$. Hence, net work done is zero.

42. (*c*) Mass percentage of solute

$$= \frac{\text{Mass of solute} \times 100}{\text{Mass of solution}}$$

Let, Mass of NaCl in 100 g solution = x g

$$0.01\% = \frac{x \times 100}{100}$$

Mass of = 0.01 g

So, in this solution 0.01 g of NaCl present in 99.99 g of water.

43. (*d*) The nucleolus is a dense-spherical dynamic membrane-less structure present in the nucleus of eukaryotic cells. Its primary function is synthesis ribosomal RNA (*r*RNA) and ribosome biogenesis.

44. (*b*) Mass (m) = 45 kg and $g = 10\,\text{m/s}^2$

Force = $m \times g$

$$F = 45 \times 10\,\text{kgm/s}^2$$

$$F = 450\,\text{kg m/s}^2$$

Area (A) = $1\,\text{cm}^2 = 10^{-4}\,\text{m}^2$

$$\text{Pressure } (P) = \frac{\text{Force } (F)}{\text{Area } (A)} = \frac{450\,\text{kg m/s}^2}{10^{-4}\,\text{m}^2}$$

$$= 450 \times 10^4\,\text{kg/ms}^2$$

$$= 4.5 \times 10^6\,\text{kg/ms}^2\ (\because 1\,\text{Pa} = 1\,\text{kg/ms}^2)$$

$$P = 4.5 \times 10^6\,\text{Pa.}$$

45. (*d*) The cell membrane or plasma membrane allows or permits the entry and exit of some materials in and out of the cell.

That's why it is also known as selectively permeable membrane.

46. (*c*) Protons → Positively charged particle.

Carbon dating → Technique to know age of fossils.

Valence electrons → Number of electrons in outermost shell.

Atomic number → Number of positively charged particles in nucleus, i.e. protons.

47. (*d*) The graph shows that the car is first at rest, then moving with non-uniform acceleration and then moving with uniform acceleration.

48. (*c*) Locust, chew or cut the plant, aphids suck the plant sap and borer, bore the stem, roots and fruits. Parthenium is a serious weed of many crops.

49. (*a*) Mass of car (m) = 800 kg

Force apply on forward direction (F_1) = 3600 N

Resistivity force (F_2) = 2000 N

Final force (F) = $F_1 - F_2$

$$F = 3600 - 2000 = 1600\,\text{N}$$

$$\text{Acceleration of car} = \frac{\text{Force}}{\text{Mass}} = \frac{1600}{800}$$

Acceleration of car = $2\,\text{m/s}^2$

50. (*c*) When water is heated, the water is converted into water vapours. These vapour have greater kinetic energy due to which pressure inside the vessel increases.

As, $pV = nRT$, the pressure is inversely proportional to volume at a constant temperature.

Practice Set 2

1. (*d*) Since, the object is covering equal distances in equal time interval, hence it is moving with a uniform velocity.

Also, $a + (n-1)\,d = 26$

$$a = 26 - (n-1)d = 26 - (9-1)2$$

$$= 26 - 16,\ a = 10$$

During Ist second, the object has already covered 10 m which shows that the object had some initial velocity.

2. (*a*) ${}^{40}_{19}X$, ${}^{39}_{19}Y$ and ${}^{40}_{20}Z$.

We can deduce from proton numbers of X, Y and Z that X and Y are same elements because they have same proton number.

3. (*b*) Both cyanobacteria and archaebacteria are prokaryotes which means they lack cell organelles and well-defined nucleus, whereas Fungi and Protista are eukaryotes and have well-defined membrane bound nucleus along with other membrane bound cell organelles. Therefore, organisms without nucleus and cell organelles belong to cyanobacteria and archaebacteria.

4. (*d*) Pressure is a scalar quantity. It depends on the magnitude of force applied and area of contact.

5. (*d*) X shows nucleus of plant and animal cells. In plant cell, it is often pushed to one side in the peripheral cytoplasm by the central vacuoles containing cell sap. It is called as the director of cell as it controls all the metabolic activities of the cell.

6. (*c*) Elements with same number of electrons (atomic number) but different number of neutrons are called isotopes. Thus, the two oxygen atoms are isotopes.

7. (*a*) Work done = Area under the F - x curve

$$= \frac{1}{2} \times 10 \times 20 = 100\text{ J}$$

8. (*b*) Kharif crops grows in rainy season and Rabi crops grow in winter season.

9. (*b*) Momentum is same.

$$\Rightarrow \quad m_1 v_1 = m_2 v_2$$

$$\Rightarrow \quad \frac{m_1}{m_2} = \frac{v_2}{v_1}$$

$$\Rightarrow \quad \frac{v_2^2}{v_1^2} = \frac{m_1^2}{m_2^2} = \frac{100}{400} = \frac{1}{4}$$

Ratio of kinetic energies, $\dfrac{1/2 m_1 v_1^2}{1/2 m_2 v_2^2} = \dfrac{10}{20} \times 4$

$$= 2:1$$

10. (*a*) 0.25 mol oxygen $\rightarrow N_A / 4$ molecules

18 g water $\rightarrow N_A$ molecules

46 g Na-atom $\rightarrow N_A \times 2$ atoms

1 mol of C-atom $\rightarrow N_A$ atoms

11. (*c*) A tendon is a white fibrous tissue which has great strength, but limited flexibility. Tendons are cord-like, strong, inelastic structures that join skeletal muscles to bones.

12. (*b*) The velocity of sound depends on the properties of the medium of propagation and the temperature of the medium.

13. (*b*) Cathode rays always travel in a straight line. Thus, if surface bends, direction of rays bends accordingly.

14. (*a*) Potential energy is the multiplication of mass (m), acceleration due to gravity (g) and height of the object. Since, height of roof is maximum.

Hence, the person will have maximum potential energy, when he is standing on roof.

15. (*a*) Randomly moving particles $\rightarrow$ Nitrogen (gas)

Layers can slide over each other $\rightarrow$ Water (liquid)

Converts into solid under pressure $\rightarrow$ Carbon dioxide (gas)

Particles are in fixed state $\rightarrow$ Sugar (solid)

16. (*a*) The loudness of a sound depends on its amplitude which depends on the force with which an object is made to vibrate. The pitch of a sound is determined by its frequency which will remain unchanged.

17. (*b*) Mitochondria is double membrane bound organelle whose outer membrane is porous and the inner membrane is deeply folded.

18. (*b*) Kinetic energy increases with increase in temperature. At A, the substance is in its solid state and at B, it starts to convert into liquid state. Now, from B to C, there is no increase in temperature and the substance goes into phase change. During a phase change, the kinetic energy of the molecules do not change. Similarly from C to D and E to F, the kinetic energy increase with increase in temperature of the substance.

19. (*a*) According to the third law of motion when the bullet is fired in forward direction, it exerts a backward push on the gun known as recoiling. Greater the mass of the gun, less will be the recoiling. Hence, the lighter rifle will hurt the shoulder more.

20. (*d*) In an area of low rainfall, farmer should prefer early maturing varieties of crops.

21. (*c*) During a circular motion, the only change in velocity is due to the change in direction of motion.

So, acceleration will be constant in magnitude and centripetal force given by $\dfrac{mv^2}{r}$ will also remain same.

22. (*a*) Number of protons = 7

Number of neutrons = 8

Number of electrons = 2 + 8 = 10

Charge = 7 − 10 = −3

Thus, symbol of the particle is N^{3-}.

23. (*c*) Pitch of sound depends on its frequency, speed of sound in air varies with temperature. Loudness of sound depends on the amplitude of vibration producing the sound. Sound travels fastest in solids and slowest in air.

24. (*c*) In unicellular organisms, vacuoles carry out the role of expelling excess water of wastes from the cell.

They also store food and water in cell and help in maintaining rigidity of cell by controlling osmosis.

25. (*d*) An airship is moving forwards at constant height when the upward and downward forces are balanced.

26. (*b*) Atomic mass of lead = 208
Atomic number of lead = 82
Number of proton (P) in lead = 82
Number of neutron (n) = Atomic mass − Number of proton
Number of neutron (n) in lead = 208 − 82 = 126
Ratio of neutron/proton in lead = 126/82
Atomic mass of bismuth = 209
Atomic number of bismuth = 83
Number of proton (p) in bismuth = 83
Number of neutron (n) in bismuth = Atomic mass − no. of proton

$$n = 209 - 83 \Rightarrow n = 126$$

Ratio of neutron/proton in bismuth = $\frac{126}{83}$

So, ratio of neutron/proton is higher in lead than bismuth.

27. (*b*) In the given figure, man got hurt because of inertia of motion upper part of body continues to be in motion in forward direction while feet come to rest as soon as they touch the road.

28. (*b*) Collenchymatous tissues have thickening at the corners which allow the bending of various parts of plant.

29. (*c*) The temperature of steam first decreases up to 100° C and at 100 °C, it becomes constant due to change in phase from gaseous to liquid. After that, if further decreases up to 0°C and here, again it becomes constant due to phase change (latent heat of fusion). After that, the temperature further decreases to −10 °C. Thus, graph (c) shows the correct temperature change with time.

30. (*b*) Specific gravity is nothing but the relative density with respect to water at 4°C.
Specific gravity of solid w.r.t liquid = 4/5
Specific gravity of liquid w.r.t water = 10/9
So, specific gravity of solid w.r.t water

$$= \frac{4}{5} \times \frac{10}{9} = \frac{8}{9}$$

Specific gravity of solid w.r.t. water = 8/9

31. (*a*) Cells are of incredible range. They vary in shapes, functions and sizes. Living organisms can be either single celled or multicelled on the basis of number of cells.
The new cells arise from pre-existing cells. The cells that are produced by cell division are exactly similar to their parent cell.
In plants, cell wall provides protection and support to the plant and also gives its actual shape.

32. (*d*) When velocity of an object decreases with time, then it is called retardation, deceleration or negative acceleration.

33. (*a*) Weight of 1 mole of X = 35 g

$$\text{Mole} = \frac{\text{Weight}}{\text{Molecular mass}}$$

$$1 = \frac{35\text{ g}}{\text{Molecular mass}}$$

Molecular mass of X = 35 g/mol
In the given compound.
X is NH_4OH (Ammonium hydroxide)
Molecular mass of $NH_4OH = 14 + 1 \times 4 + 16 + 1$
$= 14 + 4 + 16 + 1$
Molecular mass of NH_4OH = 35 g/mol.

34. (*b*) Axon is a single long conducting fibre extending from cell body in a neuron. It transmits impulse away from the cell body.

35. (*c*) Speed of wave = 340 m/s
Speed of wave (v) = wavelength × frequency
If the frequency of wave is doubled then wavelength is reduced by a factor of two and speed of the wave remains constant.

36. (*c*) Distance between the molecules of hydrogen gas increases when pressure is reduced or temperature is raised. Further, a high volume provides more space for the motion of the particles and hence, distance increases. When more hydrogen gas is added to the same container, less space is available for the motion and hence, distance decreases.

37. (*d*) The cytoplasm consists of all the contents inside the cell. Except the nucleus while the protoplasm includes the cytoplasm and the nucleus of the cell. Rest all the options are correct.

38. (*b*) Speed of sound = 330 m/s
Time taken for the hearing the echo = 8 s
Distance travelled by sound

$$= 330 \times 8 = 2640\text{ m}$$

In, 8 seconds, sound has to travel twice the distance between the mountain and Anuj.
Hence, Distance between mountain and Anuj

$$= \frac{2640}{2} = 1320\text{ m}$$

39. (*c*) They are homogeneous mixtures and also can be classified as metallic alloys. A homogeneous mixture is uniform in composition through out. White gold is a silver coloured alloy of gold with other elements.

40. (*d*) Crop rotation is growing of different crops in a pre planned succession in the same field. e.g., Rice and kiheat, sugarcane and Pea, Maise, Potato.

41. (*c*) Total distance = 1 km = 1000 m

Time taken = 1 minute = 60 s

He covers half distance (500 m) in 3/5 th of a minute

Time taken in cover 500 m = $60 \times \frac{3}{5}$ s = 36 s

Now, Remaining distance = 500 m

Remaining time = (60 − 36) s = 24 s

$$\text{Speed} = \frac{\text{distance}}{\text{time}} = \frac{500 \text{ m}}{24 \text{ s}} = 20.83 \text{ m/s}$$

42. (b) In Experiment Number 1.

The ratio of	Mass of O_2 reacted	:	Mass of H_2 reacted
	2	:	16
	1	:	8

In Experiment Number 2.

The ratio of	Mass of O_2 reacted	:	Mass of H_2 reacted
	4	:	32
	1	:	8

According to the law of constant proportions, the ratio of third experiment could be same as in above two experiments. Therefore, the mass of H_2 is 1 g and mass of O_2 used during 3rd Experiment is 8 g.

43. (*d*) The green colour of unripe fruit is due to the presence of chloroplast (plastid containing chlorophyll), when the fruit ripens, the chloroplast changes into chromoplasts (plastid) which impart colours to the ripen fruits.

44. (*a*) When a passenger tosses a coin in the moving train, the coin part of falls back because, the person is in the motion with train. So, when the train is accelerated, upper part of body of person move towards forward direction, because only lower body of person is in motion with train, so, coin falls back as shown in figure.

45. (a) I. On dissolving chalk in water, it does not dissolve completely in water. Hence, it is an example of suspension.

II. Tincture of Iodine is an antiseptic, it is also called weak iodine solution.

III. A mixture of starch in water is an example of colloidal solution.

IV. A mixture of chalk and sand is a heterogenous mixture.

V. Air is a homogenous mixture made primarily of nitrogen and oxygen.

46. (*a*) In this given diagram of cell, these arrow describes active transport against the concentration gradient. During active transport, substances move against the concentration gradient, from an area of low concentration to an area of high concentration.

This process is active, because it requires the use of energy in the form of ATP. It is the opposite of passive transport.

47. (*d*) Mass of Sonu (m) = 5 kg

Height of stairs (h) = 6.5 m and time = 7s

Power (P) = ?

We know that, $P = \frac{\text{Engery}}{\text{time}}$

Energy = mgh (g = 9.8 m/s^2)

$$\Rightarrow \quad P = \frac{mgh}{t} = \frac{5 \times 6.5 \times 9.8}{7} \Rightarrow P = \frac{318.5}{7}$$

$$\Rightarrow \quad P = 45.5 \text{ W}$$

48. (*c*) Antibacterial drugs stop the certain biochemical reaction in the bacteria that kills the bacteria. But in viruses there are a few biochemical processes which are difficult to target hence, making antiviral drugs is difficult.

49. (a) Total time taken to travel,

$$t = t_1 + t_2 + t_3 = 0.5 + 1 + 2 = 3.5 \text{ h}$$

Speeds, v_1 = 30 km/h, v_2 = 2.5 km/h

v_3 = 40 km/h

∵ Total distance = 120 km

$$\text{Average speed} = \frac{\text{Total distance}}{\text{Total time}} = \frac{120}{3.5} = 34.3 \text{ km/h}$$

50. (*b*) CO_2 molecule contains one carbon and two oxygen. Hence, three pieces would require.

H_2O_2 molecule contains 2 hydrogen and two oxygen.

Hence, 4 pieces would require.

No molecule contains one nitrogen and one oxygen. Hence, 2 pieces would require.

$C_6H_{12}O_6$ molecule contains 6 carbon, 12 hydrogen and 6 oxygen.

Hence, 24 pieces would require.